"As I read through *Uncomfortable*, I am strangely comforted. With all the talk about young Christians being disenchanted with the local church, it is refreshing to hear Brett McCracken, a Millennial, speak so affirmatively on her behalf. I am moved by Brett's grown-up perspective in these pages, a perspective that champions the church as a family not a club, a sinner's hospital not a social network, and a commitment not a consumer product. For any serious Christian, Brett's words are a wake-up call to engage—indeed, to love and devote ourselves to—this often messy, high-maintenance, painfully ordinary but also glorious, life-giving, and forever-beloved band of misfits that Jesus calls his wife. If Jesus has so tethered himself to the church, dare we untether ourselves from her? This book is a must-read."

> **Scott Sauls**, senior pastor, Christ Presbyterian Church, Nashville, Tennessee; author, *Jesus Outside the Lines*; *Befriend*; and *From Weakness to Strength*

"In a generation of dissatisfied consumers hoping to find our perfectly customized Dream Church™, Brett McCracken is the herald of a counterintuitive gospel: 'Take comfort! Church is supposed to be uncomfortable!' That's because McCracken knows it's precisely in embracing the uncomfortable truths of the gospel and immersing ourselves in the uncomfortable unity-in-diversity of the body that we are transformed into the image of Christ—the God who endured the discomfort of the cross to bring us resurrection life. In that sense, *Uncomfortable* is a sharp application of Christ's perennial call to come and die to the particular temptations of the North American church. A helpful corrective and an ultimately hopeful invitation."

> **Derek Rishmawy**, blogger, *Reformedish*; cohost, *Mere Fidelity* podcast

"As an inhabitant of the Western world, I take comfort for granted, and I like it that way. I expect to wear comfortable clothes, sleep in a comfortable bed, and have comforting food in the refrigerator. All my cultural conditioning teaches me to expect—and demand—comfort. Yet as a pastor and a disciple, I know that the demands of the gospel, while ultimately comforting, frequently are not comfortable. In this excellent book, Brett McCracken identifies and prods around many of the things that make Christian community uncomfortable: he had me itching and scratching! Brett demonstrates how rather than fleeing discomfort we need to lean into it, and in so doing find what is more deeply satisfying than the shallow comforts of our consumer age. I encourage you to read this book and embrace the itch!"

> **Matthew Hosier**, pastor, Gateway Church, Poole, United Kingdom; contributor, *thinktheology* blog

"We live in a culture oriented entirely toward comfort, and the church is not immune from its lure. Brett McCracken offers a timely and needed reminder that the call for Christians is a different one, but one that brings blessings richer than mere comfort. *Uncomfortable* will make you uncomfortable in the best of ways. Every believer needs to read this book and heed its call."

> **Karen Swallow Prior**, author, *Bc[...] Fierce Convictions: The Extraor[...] Reformer, Abolitionist*

"Ahhhh, comfort. It's the siren call to our human hearts, beckoning us to find, acquire, and maintain lives of ease. Such a bent, however, is incompatible with a vibrant Christian faith lived within a thriving Christian community. In *Uncomfortable*, Brett McCracken alerts us to the toxic ways comfort infects and hinders our faith—and how God meets our desire for comfort in gloriously unexpected ways. McCracken urges us to seek something greater than comfort: true life and true faith in Christ, found just beyond the borders of our comfort zone."

Erin Straza, author, *Comfort Detox*; managing editor, *Christ and Pop Culture*

"Americans are experts at avoiding the uncomfortable—be it awkward conversations, conflicted relationships, or lifestyle changes. But Jesus points us to a better way. In this book, McCracken shows us how the greatest glories for disciples of Jesus are often found in the most uncomfortable places his voice calls us and how the real church is not an idealized utopia beyond the fray of history, but rather Jesus powerfully present among his often muddled, messy, and awkward—yes, uncomfortable—bands of followers today."

Joshua Ryan Butler, pastor, Imago Dei Community, Portland, Oregon; author, *The Skeletons in God's Closet* and *The Pursuing God*

"Brett McCracken challenges us to face one of the greatest fears of contemporary culture: discomfort. Rather than retreating into a soothing world where everyone's 'just like me' or embracing the distractions of technology and consumerism, Brett calls us to life in community with God's people, where awkwardness, disappointment, and frustration are the norm. It's in this way of life—embracing the uncomfortable—that we'll find the richest experience of God's grace and the community our hearts truly desire. In a world where church is often just one more consumeristic choice, this is a much-needed book."

Mike Cosper, founder and director, Harbor Institute for Faith and Culture

"Anyone who looks closely at modern Christian life can see signs of the insidious self-centeredness by which we sinners are tempted to transform the gospel into something that suits our tastes and fits our plans. McCracken carries out that close examination; in fact, in this book he equips us to pursue that false comfort into all of its hiding places and root it out in Jesus's name and for the sake of the gospel."

Fred Sanders, professor of theology, Torrey Honors Institute, Biola University

"Sometimes church feels like an annoying family member you would rather see only at Thanksgiving and Christmas. We want a church that is cool and suits our tastes, not the frustrating institution that carries around the 'shame of the cross.' Brett's smoothly written book has cast all the awkwardness of church into a new and meaningful light for me. Like a Puritan voice for the cool, anti-institutional, twenty-first-century Christian, Brett charges his readers to stay and commit to the church as Christ's bride."

Emily Belz, journalist, *World* Magazine

UNCOMFORTABLE

UNCOMFORTABLE

The Awkward and Essential Challenge
of Christian Community

Brett McCracken

WHEATON, ILLINOIS

Trade paperback ISBN: 978-1-4335-5425-4
ePub ISBN: 978-1-4335-5428-5
PDF ISBN: 978-1-4335-5426-1
Mobipocket ISBN: 978-1-4335-5427-8

Library of Congress Cataloging-in-Publication Data
Names: McCracken, Brett, 1982- author.
Title: Uncomfortable: the awkward and essential challenge of Christian community / Brett McCracken.
Description: Wheaton: Crossway, 2017. | Includes bibliographical references and index.
Identifiers: LCCN 2016058581 (print) | LCCN 2017032732 (ebook) | ISBN 9781433554261 (pdf) | ISBN 9781433554278 (mobi) | ISBN 9781433554285 (epub) | ISBN 9781433554254 (tp)
Subjects: LCSH: Communities–Religious aspects–Christianity. | Interpersonal relations–Religious aspects–Christianity. | Church.
Classification: LCC BV4517.5 (ebook) | LCC BV4517.5 .M33 2017 (print) | DDC 250--dc23
LC record available at https://lccn.loc.gov/2016058581

Crossway is a publishing ministry of Good News Publishers.

LB		27	26	25	24	23	22	21	20	19	18	17
15	14	13	12	11	10	9	8	7	6	5	4	3	2	1

To the saints of Southlands Church
and the beloved Bride everywhere

Contents

Foreword

Several years ago, when I was about to speak in a seminary chapel, the seminary's president introduced me and noted that my sons were with me in the front row. He announced each of their names and asked them to stand while the congregation applauded. When he arrived at my then-three-year-old son, the service took a turn. My son—knowing the eyes in the large room were all on him—turned ashen-faced and bolted down the aisle toward the doors. I went after him, but could barely keep up. I caught him right as he was hurrying out the double doors into the sunlight outside. "Where are you going?" I asked. He, through tears, said, "I just had to get out; they were all laughing at me!" I tried to explain that the congregation was not, in fact, laughing at him, but were instead just trying to make him feel welcome. By the pull I felt as his body still leaned toward the exit, I could tell he wasn't convinced.

In truth, I kind of knew exactly what he felt. I remembered what it was like as a child to have everyone around the table singing "Happy Birthday" while they were all looking at me. I remember the sense of exposure, of uncomfortable scrutiny, that came over me. What my son and my earlier self had felt was the sense of awkwardness—of being on center stage but not knowing what to do. You may not have ever felt that way due to attention directed your way. Maybe you're the kind of extrovert who would beam at having all attention on you for a moment. But I imagine for all of you reading this page, there are moments when you feel as though you could cringe and shrink back into the shadows.

That sense of awkwardness can hinder us, in many ways, but it can also be a gift. That uncomfortable feeling can remind us that there are times when we don't know just what to say or do. It can give us a compassion for the occasional awkwardness of those around us. It can remind us that we are part of a humanity that, from our near-earliest history, found ourselves furtively hiding in the bushes from the presence of our God (Gen. 3:8–10). We often, though, want to protect ourselves from awkwardness. We want to appear to know just what to say, just what to do, just how to act—in ways that can either distinguish us or help us to blend in with whatever herd we've chosen. Sometimes that self-protection means deflecting the very reality—presence and relatedness—that can draw us out of ourselves and toward wholeness. The intense moment, the "I love you" or the "I am concerned about you" or the "Here's what you mean to me" moment, becomes deflected with a joke or a change of subject. Sometimes it is not comfortable to be loved—especially if you don't believe you are worth loving.

This book, by one of the country's most gifted and respected young writers, shines the uncreated light of the gospel onto our most awkward and uncomfortable hiding places. This book demonstrates how the Christian gospel and the Christian community undo our sense of the "privacy" of our lives, moving issue-by-issue through some of the most challenging areas of belief and practice. This book is solidly evangelical in the best sense of that word—anchored to the gospel and embedded with the invitation to find life and rest in the crucified Christ Jesus. I plan to give away many copies of this book, especially to those who are new to the gospel, furtively starting to feel their way around in what can seem to be a strange new subculture.

As you read this book, I would challenge you to ask yourself where you feel uncomfortable. Where do you wish to deflect the attention of the biblical witness, of God himself? Asking those questions might prompt you to turn those areas over in concentrated prayer, or they might spur you to seek help from those in your church community. At the very least, these questions will help you to see that you are not alone. Our sense of awkwardness—however pronounced and however frequently experienced—really isn't our problem. Our problem is that we live in a culture of comfort and conformity—a culture from which the kingdom of God calls us into a new creation that seems upside-down in comparison. Our problem, in this time-between-the-times, is that we rarely feel uncomfortable enough. This book can help us.

Russell Moore

My Dream Church

As you come to him, a living stone rejected by men but in the sight of God chosen and precious, you yourselves like living stones are being built up as a spiritual house, to be a holy priesthood, to offer spiritual sacrifices acceptable to God through Jesus Christ.

1 PETER 2:4-5

Those who love their dream of a Christian community more than they love the Christian community itself become destroyers of that Christian community even though their personal intentions may be ever so honest, earnest and sacrificial.

DIETRICH BONHOEFFER

If you could dream up the perfect church, what would it look like?

On days when I'm sitting in my real church and feeling frustrated by something, I sometimes daydream about my *ideal* church: the one where I would feel completely understood, where my perspectives would be valued, where my gifts and passions would flourish. I dream about a church I would always be proud (and never embarrassed) to call home; a church so amazing that any non-Christian who visited would never want to leave.

My hypothetical dream church would look something like the following. (If you'd prefer to skip over my self-indulgent dream church description, simply turn to page 23 to resume the actual argument of this book.)

The Building

My dream church (hereafter simply called DC) would be located in a major world city, in a neighborhood with ethnic, cultural, and class diversity.

DC would be architecturally contemporary and minimalist, environmentally sustainable (LEED-certified), with nods to classic church aesthetics. DC would be celebrated as a forward-thinking example of responsible urban design and sacred space, elegantly balancing practicality with superfluous beauty. The church's sanctuary would be the architectural focal point and have such great acoustics and layout that it would become a desirable venue for concerts, arts, and community events.

Included in the church building would be a small number of offices and classrooms, a large all-purpose room, a bookstore, and a fitness center. A small green space on the church's property would include a community garden growing a variety of organic produce. As part of the church's energy-efficient design, its roof would also be green, featuring herb gardens and prayer spaces.

In addition to the main church building, members of DC would own and operate a highly rated restaurant, coffee shop, and roastery in the building next door, featuring ingredients from the church's gardens.

Mercy Ministries and Community Outreach

DC would be a church very much about demonstrating the transformative power of the gospel through mercy, justice, and outreach efforts. Some of these efforts would be entirely church-driven, but many of them would be partnerships for the common good with local nonprofit and civic organizations.

All church members (including middle school and high school youth) would participate in one or more service opportunities for the community, such as: local food banks, after-school tutoring, nursing home visitation, crisis pregnancy centers, women's shelters, or anti-trafficking task forces. In partnership with a local rescue mission, DC's restaurant kitchen would cook free community meals on select weeknights, and the church would open its all-purpose room on several nights a week as an emergency homeless shelter.

As one of the city's finest musical venues, DC's beautiful church sanctuary would be rented out multiple nights a week as a concert venue. The church's public arts and community events committee would organize the venue's calendar with lectures, concerts, and film screenings year round. The church's sanctuary would be a vibrant hub of the city's civic life and arts scene.

Additionally, DC's lobby would serve as a community art space where artists from both inside and outside the church could display and sell their work. DC's bookstore would sell Bibles and books but also artisan goods made by church and community members, as well as coffee beans from the adjacent roastery and single-varietal jams made from the church's organic garden. A percentage of sales from these goods would go toward DC's mercy and justice fund.

The church's adjacent restaurant and coffee shop would also play an integral role in community outreach. Open all week, these eateries would provide community dining and study spaces as well as venues for poetry readings and concerts. The restaurant/coffee shop's kitchen and wait staff would be partially funneled from a local job training organization that helps homeless people, ex-convicts, and unemployed people develop skills to earn a living.

DC's fully equipped fitness center would provide another service to the community, offering various fitness classes, CrossFit, and personal training throughout the week at rates cheaper than typical gym memberships.

DC's all-purpose room and classrooms would be open periodically for outreach classes during the week, including Alpha for skeptics with questions about Christianity; Celebrate Recovery groups for those struggling with addictions; and a six-week premarital course offered a few times a year for seriously dating or engaged couples.

Theology

Theologically, DC would be conservative and Reformed, though not afraid to preach and celebrate the best contributions of Wesleyan and Pentecostal theology and even the occasional Eastern Orthodox or Catholic thinker (not to mention N. T. Wright!). The church would be thoroughly gospel-centered, Spirit-led, and missionally minded. Both the five *Solas* and the charismatic gifts would be inescapable in the church's day-to-day life. A portrait of Martyn Lloyd-Jones would hang prominently in one of the church offices.

Structurally, DC would be elder-led, with preaching alternating between elders and a few non-elders with preaching gifts. Paid staff would be minimal as the church membership's high volunteer percentage would bear the load of most all programs and functions of the church.

Though Word-centric, DC would have a robust theology of the Holy Spirit and balance the tensions therein. Other things DC would hold in healthy tension: local and global mission, engaging the culture with truth and love, preaching the gospel and demonstrating it in deed.

Multiplication and church planting would be central to DC's mission. Member growth (mostly from new converts through outreach programs like Alpha) would lead not to new buildings or bigger sanctuaries, but to new church plants. As part of its church-planting orientation, DC would be part of a global network of church-planting partners, resulting in close relationships with churches both domestically and internationally. This would afford DC frequent opportunities to send and receive ministry teams for mutual building up and encouragement. New churches would be planted out of these partnerships and networks rather than solely relying on DC's resources and members.

DC would have a robust, Kuyperian theology of vocation and an intellectual bent appropriate to its urban context. Except for a bit more on the Holy Spirit, the "Vision and Values" section of Tim Keller's Redeemer Presbyterian sums up DC's theology pretty well.[1]

Sundays

A typical Sunday morning at DC would begin in the lobby with coffee and pastries (chocolate blackberry croissants, maple bacon biscuits, lemon pistachio polenta cake, and so on) from the adjacent roastery and restaurant.

Worship services would incorporate liturgy and creeds, confession, read and spontaneous prayer, an exchanging of "the peace," thirty to forty-five minutes of preaching, instrumental music, and extended singing time before and after the preaching.

Music on stage would be minimalist by modern evangelical church standards, with largely acoustic bands of fewer than five musicians. Piano, acoustic guitar, string trios, and French horn would be regularly incorporated, as would a variety of music styles from other cultures and contexts. A beautiful pipe organ (cherished not only by the elderly congregants) would figure prominently into at least one hymn each Sunday. Musicians would also be encouraged to write, record, and perform original music, largely inspired by biblical poetry and the Psalter.

Sunday morning services would always incorporate communion, with congregants standing and taking the elements collectively as an elder spoke the corresponding liturgy. Each Sunday morning would also end with a time of response, prayer, and a clear call to conversion. Planned and spontaneous baptisms would take place regularly, as multiple conversions would be a weekly occurrence.

Following services, churchgoers would be invited to stay for a community lunch in the all-purpose room. Catered by the adjacent restaurant and prominently featuring the best of the church garden's seasonal produce, these lunches would often last for hours and hours, featuring wine and laughter, bocce ball games on the lawn, tea and scones on the roof, walks around town, or naps on the couches by the fireplace (there would be a fireplace reading room somewhere, complete with a collection of single-malt scotches made available for consumption at the behest of a responsible-but-not-stingy elder entrusted with the keys to the liquor cabinet).

Most members would stay at church for large parts of the day on Sunday along with their non-Christian friends and spiritually seeking acquaintances, as there really would be no more welcoming, relaxing, beautifully diverse, and heaven-like place to be in the city.

Discipleship and Community Life

During DC's corporate worship service on Sunday morning, children through grade five would have classes of their own, although they would all participate in the singing portion of "big church" once a month. Middle school and high school students would be with the whole church on Sunday morning but would have their own gathering after the community lunch. During this time, adult education classes in Bible, theology, and apologetics would be offered in cooperation with a nearby evangelical seminary.

Church membership and assimilation would be an emphasis of DC. A robust catechism course would be required for new believers and a membership class for new members. Requirements for membership would include taking the class, joining a small group, volunteering for a serve team (see following), and tithing regularly. Small group, volunteering, and tithing participation would all be near 100 percent, and the church's budget (half of which would go to church planting/missions and mercy/justice) would thrive accordingly.

Each church member would volunteer for one of the following serve teams:

- **Food and Hospitality:** the restaurant, coffee shop, organic garden, community lunches, meal trains, hosting out-of-town guests, and anything else involving food and hospitality.
- **Prayer:** pre-service prayer meetings on Sunday mornings, prayer for people during and after each service, prayer walks, prayer newsletters, the rooftop prayer garden, and more.
- **Education and Outreach:** adult education, children's and youth classes, new-believer catechism, nursery, small groups, Kuyper clubs (see below), Alpha, etc.
- **Assimilation:** greeting people on Sunday mornings, visitor information, follow-up, membership classes, helping newcomers find ways to get involved.
- **Operations:** technical and facility needs, groundskeeping, media/AV, room setup, lighting, stage management, etc.
- **Music and Arts:** music ministries of the church (including weeknight Evensong services), public arts and community events committee, lobby art gallery curating.
- **Mercy and Justice:** organizing partnerships and administrative needs related to mercy and justice initiatives, helping church members serve the common good of the city.
- **Communications:** church website, social media, emails, member database, printed bulletins, and branding.
- **Community Care:** connecting relationally gifted members of the community to the counseling and mentoring needs of the church with a focus on intergenerational discipleship and soul care.

Church members would also be encouraged to join a "Kuyper Club"[2] as a way to deepen community and invite nonbelieving friends to a variety of interest-based, mid-week activities. These clubs would include things like:

- **Inklings 2.0:** A writer's workshop for the literarily inclined
- **Taste and See:** For foodies to explore the local restaurant scene
- **Holy Spirits:** For those who like to sample rare scotch, bourbon, rum, and other spirits
- **Singles Supper Club:** Where singles gather to cook and enjoy a feast together
- **Running the Race:** Training group for aspiring runners of 10Ks, half marathons, and marathons
- **CrossFit:** A CrossFit club which meets in the church's fitness center
- **Creation Appreciation:** A hiking, backpacking, and camping club
- **Augustine Society:** A reading group focused on the church fathers and historical theology
- **Robinson Society:** A reading group focused on twentieth- and twenty-first-century fiction
- **Rothko Society:** Takes regular trips to art exhibits and engages the city's art scene
- **Malick Society:** Watches and discusses movies (not just by Terrence Malick!) from the perspective of Christian faith
- **Eliot Society:** A poetry reading and writing group

In addition to these forums for discipleship and community life, DC would also own several homes and apartments in the city that would be rented out to members in the church as a way of building intentional community. These houses would focus on spiritual formation but also outreach and service, partnering with some of the aforementioned mercy and justice initiatives.

Always mindful of not becoming too large or too insular, DC would also have a robust leadership and church-planting training process whereby capable and trustworthy leaders would be constantly developed and sent to serve in new church plants or existing partner churches both locally and globally.

My Dream Is Not the Point

I'd be lying if I said that DC description wasn't enjoyable to write. In fact, I could have kept going. I didn't even get into my ideal color palette for the church's website (organic shades of black, olive, and tan) or my preference for prelude music (pipe organ version of Radiohead's "Everything in Its Right Place"). But you get the idea, and I'm sure you've had enough. There are few things more annoying than reading through *someone else's* subjective vision of "the perfect church."

I am a bit disgusted with how easy it is to describe in such detail my hypothetical "dream church." It's easy because this is how we've been conditioned to think. "Have it your way" consumerism is the air we breathe.

We curate our social feeds so that everything we see befits our tastes and leanings. If a Tweet annoys us, we unfollow that Twitterer. On Netflix we populate "My List" with all that our over-mediated hearts desire. If we start a movie and the first ten minutes are boring, we remove it from the list and forget about it forever. Consumerism is about unlimited choice and unlimited speed. We choose exactly what we want, take only what we want from it, and move on.

This mind-set has infiltrated the way we approach church: as a thing we can design according to our checklist of preferences. And if a church stops catering to our desires or makes us uncomfortable (the pastor says something disagreeable, worship music becomes too saccharine, someone speaks in tongues), we move on. There are dozens of other options in town.

Consumerism is chronic dissatisfaction. We're always on the quest for more and better, hoping for new heights of satisfaction. The "dream church" is always a potential out there; the grass is always greener at the trendy new church in town.

What We Want Is Not What We Need

The point of this introduction—and the point of this book—is that we must debunk and destroy this toxic consumerist approach. It's bad for our physical health and worse for our spiritual health.

If we always approach church through the lens of wishing this or that were different, or longing for a church that "gets me" or "meets me where I'm at," we'll never commit anywhere (or, Protestants that we are, we'll just start our own church). But church shouldn't be about being perfectly understood and met in our comfort zone; it should be about understanding God more, and meeting him where *he* is. This is an uncomfortable but beautiful thing. As nineteenth-century preacher Charles Spurgeon once said:

> If I had never joined a church till I had found one that was perfect, I should never have joined one at all; and the moment I did join it, if I had found one, I should have spoiled it, for it would not have been a perfect church after I had become a member of it. Still, imperfect as it is, it is the dearest place on earth to us.[3]

What we think we want from a church is almost never what we need. However challenging it may be to embrace, God's idea of church is far more glorious than any dream church we could conjure. It's not about finding a church that perfectly fits my theological, architectural, or political preferences. It's about becoming like "living stones" that are "being built up as a spiritual house" focused on and held together by Jesus, the stone the builders rejected who became the cornerstone (1 Pet. 2:4–7).

Contrary to the wisdom of consumerism, we're better off giving up the "dream church" ideal and the "perfect fit" fallacy. I've seen this firsthand in my current church experience in Brea, California. Whether because of its music (louder and more contemporary than my tastes), its emphasis on spontaneous prayer in "groups of three or four around you" (I'm an introvert), or its openness to the wildness of the Holy Spirit (I grew up Southern Baptist), much about the church makes me uncomfortable. It's far from the "dream church" that meets all my preferred checkboxes. Yet in this not-my-dream church, my wife and I have grown immensely and been used by God. Its community has shown me clearly that "how it fits me" is the wrong criteria for finding the right church.

Rather, church should be about collectively spurring one another to "be fit" to the likeness of Christ (Ephesians 4–5). And this can happen in almost any sort of church as long as it's fixed on Jesus, anchored in the gospel, and committed to the authority of Scripture.

Instead of *à la carte* Christianity driven by fickle tastes and "dream church" appetites, what if we learned to love churches even when—or perhaps because—they challenge us and stretch us out of our comfort zones? Instead of driving twenty miles away to attend a church that "fits my needs," what if we committed to the nearest nonheretical, Bible-believing church where we could grow and serve—and where Jesus is the hero—however uncomfortable it may be?[4]

Commitment even amidst discomfort, faithfulness even amidst disappointment: this is what being the people of God has always been about. Imagine if Yahweh had bailed on Israel the minute they said or did something offensive, opting instead to "shop around" for a new people (Canaanites? Philistines? Egyptians?). Imagine if God were as fickle and restless as we are. But he isn't. God's covenant faithfulness to his people, even when the relationship is difficult and embarrassing, should be instructive to us. A healthy relationship with the local church is like a healthy marriage: it only works when grounded in selfless commitment and a nonconsumerist covenant.

Is this approach uncomfortable, awkward, and stretching? Absolutely. But that is the point.

———

This book is about the comforting gospel of Jesus Christ that leads us to live uncomfortable lives for him. It's about recovering a willingness to do hard things, to embrace hard truths, to do life with hard people for the sake and glory of the One who did the hardest thing.

Each chapter of this book will explore an "uncomfortable" aspect of becoming the church Jesus wants us to be:

- **Embrace the Discomfort:** Christians who seek growth should embrace, rather than fear or disown, the difficult aspects of following Jesus.
- **The Uncomfortable Cross:** What does it mean that a macabre execution device is the central symbol of our faith? What does it look like to embrace suffering and sacrifice?
- **Uncomfortable Holiness:** Christians are called to be a set-apart people, pursuing values different than the world around them. This involves the uncomfortable but essential process of pursuing holiness and not settling for mere *authenticity*.
- **Uncomfortable Truths:** Following Jesus means accepting truths that are uncomfortable in today's world, whether it be a biblical sexual ethic, the reality of hell, the idea that the universe was created, or any number of other unfashionable things.
- **Uncomfortable Love:** Jesus calls his followers not only to love truth but also to love others, radically. Christlike love doesn't just look like the passivity of *niceness* or *tolerance*. It is active, uncomfortable, and unconditional.
- **Uncomfortable Comforter:** Jesus gives Christians the Holy Spirit as a *paraclete*, a "Comforter" to indwell us, guide us into truth, and grow in him. But for many Christians the role of the Spirit is a source of controversy and unease.
- **Uncomfortable Mission:** Christianity would be a lot more comfortable if we could just keep to ourselves and mind our own business. But we are called to mission, to tirelessly serve others and evangelize, which is not easy.
- **Uncomfortable People:** People are flawed and weird and self-serving; it's a wonder any of us get along. And yet for Christians striving to be the church, overcoming "people problems" and bearing with one another in love is essential.

- **Uncomfortable Diversity:** It's uncomfortable doing church with people who are very different from us. But unity amidst diversity is one of the greatest testaments to the power of the gospel. It's an uncomfortable thing we must strive for.
- **Uncomfortable Worship:** Everyone has a preference about style of worship music, prayer, liturgy, etc. Yet putting aside personal preferences and embracing unified, God-centric worship is part of what it means to follow Jesus together.
- **Uncomfortable Authority:** Reluctance to submit to authority is the reason many people abandon church or create their own custom spirituality. Yet Christianity would be chaos without the guardrails of authority.
- **Uncomfortable Unity:** The challenge and messiness of unity in the body of Christ will be increasingly urgent as the need for partnership and mutual support among the "Christian remnant" becomes greater.
- **Uncomfortable Commitment:** The perfect church does not exist, but committing to a church in spite of its flaws is essential—and worth it. Churchless Christianity is an oxymoron.
- **Countercultural Comfort:** There is comfort for those who follow Jesus, but not in the sense that a consumer society defines comfort.

Are you willing to lay aside your "dream church" consumer fantasies and accept the hard-to-stomach truths and awkward requirements of locking arms with weird people in common pursuit of Jesus? Are you willing to relinquish your freedom to do and be whatever you want? Are you willing to embrace persecution when it comes, to "count everything as loss because of the surpassing worth of knowing Christ Jesus my Lord" (Phil. 3:8)?

If so, or maybe if you aren't quite there yet, this book is for you. It may be uncomfortable, but it will be worth it. On the other side of discomfort is delight in Christ.

PART 1

UNCOMFORTABLE FAITH

1

Embrace the Discomfort

Whoever loves his life loses it, and whoever hates his life in this world will keep it for eternal life.

JOHN 12:25

We must put away our convenient notions of God—the one who always agrees with us, the one who always favors our nation or political agenda, the one who feeds us candy and never vegetables.

ADAM MCHUGH

There was at least a four-year gap between when I prayed to ask Jesus to be my Savior, and when I publicly confessed him as such in my church and asked to be baptized. That's how much of an introvert I am.

It was one thing to pray to Jesus in private; quite another to *go forward* during an altar call. For a shy kid, the latter was terrifying: standing up, stepping out of the pew, walking up that intimidating aisle, finding the right words to say to the pastor who wore cowboy boots with his suits. The thought of doing it made me sweat. Literally.

For years I dreaded the invitation time in the Sunday services of our little Baptist church in Oklahoma. During the inevitable one or two verses of "Just as I Am" or "Softly and Tenderly," when the pastor beckoned anyone to come forward who felt convicted to "confess with your mouth that Jesus is Lord" (Rom. 10:9; this verse terrified me), I sat in turmoil, clearly convicted but unwilling to take the uncomfortable step. I often felt sick to my stomach during these moments of the church service (and not just because of the mayonnaise-based casseroles that dominated our church's potlucks). This went on for years. After one particularly nerve-wracking Sunday night service (I'm sure the sermon was out of Revelation), I actually ran to the church bathroom and threw up.

When at age ten I finally moved from my seat to go forward during the altar call, it was indeed uncomfortable. I remember tapping my dad's shoulder and whispering to him that I wanted to go forward, but would he walk up there with me? He did. I told the pastor I'd asked Jesus to be my Savior and wanted to be baptized. My decision was announced to the congregation, and a few weeks later I was awkwardly dunked in lukewarm water. All of it was uncomfortable, but not nearly as bad as my worrying mind had imagined. And thanks be to God, my altar call stomachaches ended that day, once and for all.

The "God of all comfort" (2 Cor. 1:3) filled me with a new-found peace at that moment, but it was by no means the end of discomfort on my Jesus-following journey. There have been, and continue to be, aspects of Christianity that make me uncomfortable. Most of them have to do with living out the faith in the way Jesus mandated: not as individuals but as a fellowship—as the church. And church is hard.

Here are just a few of the things that have proven awkward and/or uncomfortable for me in my three decades of church-going life:

- Praying aloud in public—introverts reading this will understand

- Speaking on stage or from any sort of podium, for any reason
- That moment in a worship song when everyone is sitting, and then as the song builds to a climax, people start popping up around you and you feel pressured to stand up too
- That moment in a small group or church meeting when the leader asks if someone will close in prayer, everyone avoids eye contact, and you just KNOW he will call on you
- The meet-and-greet portion of church where small talk with strangers is encouraged
- Men's ministry activities involving sports, meat, and people who call you "boss"
- Door-to-door or street evangelism (or any sort of evangelism, really)
- Holding sweaty hands with strangers during a prayer circle time that never seems to end
- Youth group

There is more I could list, of course, but as much as it makes me cringe to think of it all, it also fills me with joy. For it is on account of the uncomfortable, the awkward, the difficult, and the challenging that I have grown. This is as true for life in general as it is for the life of faith.

If I had never taken the awkward and vulnerable step of asking Kira on that first date to the local Thai restaurant in 2010, and if I hadn't then been OK that she needed time (six months!) before she was really ready to start dating, she would not be my wife today.

If every day Kira and I shut our doors and kept our home a quiet haven of solitude (my preference), we would miss out on the benefits of living hospitably and learning from the beautiful souls who sit at our table and on our couches each week.

If I had listened to my introverted instincts every time I was offered a public-speaking opportunity or a teaching gig, I would have missed out on amazing opportunities to share with, shape, and engage hundreds of people.

We grow most when we are outside of our comfort zones.

We are more effective when we are on the edge of risk.

We hold beliefs more dear and pursue goals more passionately when they are accompanied by a cost.

This is why I believe Christians ought to embrace, rather than avoid, the necessity of grounding their faith in a local church context, however uncomfortable, awkward, and frustrating it may be.

And it's why I believe churches ought to embrace, rather than avoid, the uncomfortable aspects of Christianity if they are to thrive in the twenty-first century.

There is a reverse correlation between the comfortability of Christianity and its vibrancy. When the Christian church is comfortable and cultural, she tends to be weak. When she is uncomfortable and countercultural, she tends to be strong.

I believe the latter is how she was meant to be.

The Dying-Away of Cultural Christianity

The number of people in the United States who call themselves Christians is shrinking. And that's a good thing.

Every few years, new data shows an ongoing decline of Americans who identify as Christians and an ongoing rise in those who identify as religiously unaffiliated (the "nones"). Yet headlines announcing the death of American Christianity are misleading and premature.

"Christianity isn't collapsing; it's being clarified," wrote Ed Stetzer in 2015 following the release of Pew Research data showing the Christian share of the American population declined almost eight percentage points from 2007 to 2014. Stetzer points out that the surge in "nones" is because nominal Christians are giving up the pretense of faith while convictional Christians remain committed.[1]

For most of US history, to be *American* was to be "Christian." National identity was conflated with religious identity in a way that produced a distorted form of Christianity, mostly about family values, Golden Rule moralism, and good citizenship. The God of this "Christianity" was first and foremost a nice guy who rewarded moral living by sanctifying the American dream: life, liberty, and the pursuit of happiness (i.e., a substantial 401(k), a three-car garage, and as many Instagram followers as possible). This form of Christianity—prominent in twenty-first-century America—has been aptly labeled "Moralistic Therapeutic Deism," a faith defined by a distant, "cosmic ATM" God who only cares that we are nice to one another and feel good about ourselves.[2]

This faux God—stripped of theological and historical specificity and closer to Santa Claus than Yahweh—began to flourish amidst the gradual "death of God" narrative advanced by philosophical, literary, artistic, and scientific elites from the Enlightenment to postmodernity. In this context, mainstream Christianity became less about truly believing in God and supernatural events like the incarnation and resurrection; it became more about the rites and rituals of Christianity-flavored morality: a convenient, comfortable, quaint system of personal and societal uplift. Thankfully, and predictably, this sort of toothless, "nice," good-citizen Christianity is on the decline. Why? As Terry Eagleton observes, it's because Christianity is fundamentally disruptive rather than conciliatory to polite society and powers-that-be:

> The form of life Jesus offers his followers is not one of social integration but a scandal to the priestly and political establishment. It is a question of being homeless, propertyless, peripatetic, celibate, socially marginal, disdainful of kinsfolk, averse to material possessions, a friend of outcasts and pariahs, a thorn in the side of the Establishment and a scourge of the rich and powerful.[3]

What we are seeing in American Christianity is a healthy pruning away of the mutant and neutered forms of it that are easily abandoned when they become culturally inconvenient or unfashionable. As Russell Moore observes, "A Christianity that reflects its culture, whether that culture is Smith College or NASCAR, only lasts as long as it is useful to its host. That's because it's, at root, idolatry, and people turn from their idols when they stop sending rain."[4]

Rather than being a cause for alarm, the dying-away of cultural Christianity should be seen as an opportunity. It used to be too easy to be a Christian in America; so easy that one could adopt the label simply by being born in this "Christian nation" and going to church once or twice a year (if that), in between relentless attempts to swindle the stock market, accumulate beach properties, and build an empire of wealth and acclaim.

To be sure, and especially in contrast to much of the rest of the world, it's still easy to be a Christian in America. But it is becoming less easy and certainly less *normal*. And that's a good thing. Christianity, founded on belief in the supernatural resurrection of a first-century Jewish carpenter, has been and always will be *abnormal*. Again, Russell Moore:

> The Book of Acts, like the Gospels before it, shows us that Christianity thrives when it is, as Kierkegaard put it, a sign of contradiction. Only a strange gospel can differentiate itself from the worlds we construct. But the strange, freakish, foolish old gospel is what God uses to save people and to resurrect churches (1 Cor. 1:20–22).[5]

Following Christ is not one's golden ticket to a white-picket-fence American dream. It's an invitation to die, to pick up a cross. Christians are those who give themselves away in love and sacrifice to advance a kingdom that is not of this world (John 18:36).

As C. S. Lewis writes: "I didn't go to religion to make me happy. I always knew a bottle of Port would do that. If you want a religion to make you feel really comfortable, I certainly don't recommend Christianity."[6]

Christianity Should Be Uncomfortable

In the face of growing secularization and the decline of cultural/nominal Christianity in the West, the Christianity that will survive will be the kind that doesn't shrink from discomfort or apologize for the increasingly countercultural things it calls people to believe and do.

At a time when young Americans are ever less familiar with Jesus and the Christian gospel, and the spiritual-but-not-religious mantra is ever more proliferate, this sort of *real* Christianity will be clearer and more urgent. The Western world doesn't need a more muddled, confused, "I love Jesus but not the church" Christianity made up of a million different opinions and to-each-his-own permutations. Rather, it needs a true, unified, and eloquent witness to the distinctly alternative vision for life that Jesus offers. And this will only come with a renewed commitment to the local church in all of its uncomfortable but life-giving glory.

Nominal Christianity and Moralistic Therapeutic Deism will gradually die off. We should expedite their passing. One way we can do this is by rallying around the true, costly pursuit of Christ as believers committed to the imperfect but essential local church. Not only will this help distinguish true from *almost* Christianity, but it will renew and revive our churches. It will result in a stronger, more sustainable, more identifiable (and I think more united) Christianity. It will make congregations more mature and effective, because those who remain will be all in, committed, and invested.

Anyone who has ever grown in a skill—a sport, an art form, a job—knows that growth doesn't come by way of comfort. Growth happens when we push ourselves outside of our comfort zone and allow our confidence and assumptions to be shaken. Those unwilling to stay the uncomfortable course simply quit. These people are not the ones who win medals or create art of lasting significance. They are not the ones who build the church. No, the builders and changers of this world are the ones who put their comfort aside for the sake of something greater.

Giving Up "Dream Church" and Embracing Discomfort

The "dream church" picture I painted in the introduction looks very little like the church, Southlands, where I am now a member.

Southlands is nondenominational, meets in a renovated prosthetics factory, and has only the slightest liturgical bent. It's Reformed-ish but Holy Spirit focused, with impromptu "words" from the congregation and quiet prayer in tongues a common occurance. The music is relentlessly loud. To be honest, the worship services often make me quite uncomfortable.

And I'm OK with that. I love my church.

Talking about one's personal "dream church" is an exercise in not only futility but flat-out gospel denial. The church does not exist to meet our "comfort zone" preferences but rather to destabilize them, to jostle us awake from the dead-eye stupor of a culture of comfort-worship that impedes our growth.

Attending my current church has been difficult and full of personal discomfort, but also probably the most spiritually enriching churchgoing season of my life. Nothing matures you quite like faithfulness amid discomfort.

For too long the consumer logic of Christian culture has been: Find a church that meets your needs! Find a church where the worship music moves you, the pastor's preaching compels you, and the homogenous community welcomes you! You, you, you!

But this model doesn't work. Not only is it coldly transactional (what have you done for me lately?) and devoid of covenantal commitment (consumerist church attendance is basically a celebrity marriage without a prenup), it's also anti-gospel. A true gospel community is not about convenience and comfort and chai lattes in the vestibule. It's about pushing each other forward in holiness and striving together for the kingdom, joining along in the ongoing work of the Spirit in this world. Those interested only in their comfort and happiness need not apply. Being the church is difficult.

The thing is, many young people today resonate with this. They're sick of being sold spiritual comfort food. They want to be part of something that has forward momentum and doesn't slow down so that a few fickle, FOMO ("fear of missing out") Millennials can decide whether or not they want to get on board. They want a community that is so compelled by the gospel and so confident in Christ that they pay little heed to target demographics and CNN articles about what twentysomethings are saying today about their "dream church." As one popular book written by Christian Millennials suggests, there is "a growing movement of Christian young people who are rebelling against the low expectations of their culture by choosing to 'do hard things' for the glory of God."[7]

College students I know are not interested in a church with a nice, shiny college ministry. They want a church that is alive, bearing fruit, and making disciples. The young professionals in our life group do not meet week after week because hanging out with a diverse array of awkward personalities after a long day's work makes their lives easier. No. They come because there is growth when believers in community help each other look outside of themselves and to Jesus.

Looking outside of ourselves. Putting aside personal comfort and coming often to the cross. This is what being the church means.

It means worshiping all together without segregating by age or interest (e.g., "contemporary" or "traditional"). It means preaching the whole counsel of God, even the unpopular bits. It means fighting against homogeneity and cultivating diversity as much as possible, even if this makes people uncomfortable. It means prioritizing the values of church membership and tithing, even if it turns people off. It means pushing back against the privatization of relationships by insisting that the health of marriages is the business of the church family. It means sticking around even when the church goes through hard times. It means building a tight-knit community, but not an insular one, that engages the surrounding community and sends out members when mission calls them away. It means bearing with one another in love on matters of debate and yet not shying away from discipline. It means preaching truth and love in tension, even when the culture calls it bigotry.

None of this is easy, and none of it is comfortable. But by the grace of God and with the Holy Spirit's help, uncomfortable church can become something we treasure.

The Remnants and Legacy of Comfortable Christianity

I have never lived in a place where being a Christian was abnormal or especially difficult. Born and raised in the Bible Belt, my Christianity was shaped by the values of the heartland (Tulsa, Oklahoma; Shawnee, Kansas; and Wheaton, Illinois). Going to church was just something you did. Evangelical Christianity was so mainstream that the Power Team put on assemblies in my public middle school and the DJ played DC Talk's "Jesus Freak" at prom. Though things have changed a bit since my childhood, the Midwest is still very much a hotbed of cultural Christianity. Churches may be slightly emptier these days, but God, family, and country are still the predominant values of the region.

These days I live in Orange County, California, which is not exactly the Bible Belt but has nevertheless been an incubator of evangelical trends for at least the last half century. In a way, Orange County is the poster child for comfortable Christianity. This is, after all, where the church-growth and seeker-sensitive movements were perfected and mass distributed to the rest of evangelicalism.

Orange County is a center of business and wealth, and also a center of pleasure: sun, fun, shopping, consumerism. It's no surprise that Christianity has been framed through these lenses here. The megachurch, seeker-sensitive Christianity that emerged here, and came to define American evangelicalism in the 1990s and 2000s, was driven by the idea that church should pay attention to consumer desires. Churches should construct their spaces, their worship styles, and their preaching to be as friendly, inoffensive, and appealing as possible to the "seeker."

Admirably evangelistic, this approach resulted in huge numbers and growth for many churches. Who doesn't want to attend a church where single-origin Ethiopian Yirgacheffe coffee, U2-sounding rock music, and Ted Talk–caliber preaching can be experienced in under one hour, with no "Softly and Tenderly" altar calls anywhere in sight?

But the seeker-sensitive movement didn't do much to combat the mutations of cultural Christianity; in many cases, it reinforced them. Sadly, Moralistic Therapeutic Deism thrived in the youth groups of many a megachurch. Shorn of meaty theology and the cruciform cost of following Jesus, the seeker-sensitive ethos emphasized "your best life now" self-help that sold church as little more than a family-friendly support group and social club full of Hollister-wearing teenagers driving Audis and Camaros.

Yet framing Christianity as a product to be sold to a customer (who is always right) is disingenuous to the actual call of Christ and deadly to the prospects of a thriving, transformative, gospel-witnessing church community.

The early church recognized this. It was very different from the seeker-sensitive, low-barrier-to-entry churches of today. In the first centuries of Christianity, churches were hard to enter. And this was a key to their growth. As one scholar observes, "They didn't grow because of their cultural accessibility; they grew because they required commitment to an unpopular God who didn't require people to perform cultic acts correctly but instead equipped them to live in a way that was richly unconventional."[8]

Today the seeker-sensitive approach takes the form of the radically individualistic *iChurch*, which is all about *what church does for me* and has little tolerance for covenantal commitment or accountability. Naturally, iChurch transitions eventually to *no-Church*, which is precisely the nominal-to-none trajectory we are now seeing.

In the wake of the church-growth movement and seeker-sensitive evangelicalism, we must acknowledge that the Christianity we need, *the only Christianity that will survive*, will probably not pack out megachurches and likely not spawn bestsellers. Why? Because it will be gospel-sensitive and seeker-insensitive.

It will be true Christianity.

Seeker-Insensitive: The Uncomfortable Call of Following Christ

Being a follower of Jesus brings immeasurable rewards, to be sure. Jesus came so that we could have abundant life (John 10:10) and so that our souls would find rest (Matt. 11:29). Next to the burdens we place on ourselves to justify our own existence and to live up to the cultural standards of "success," what Jesus offers is grace upon grace: "My yoke is easy, and my burden is light" (Matt. 11:30). Choosing Jesus is choosing resurrection, freedom, redemption, salvation, and eternal life. We musn't forget this. Christianity is not a faith of self-loathing, fetishizing persecution, and adopting a martyrdom complex. Christianity is not about seeking out suffering; it's about seeking first the kingdom of God. It's not about celebrating our pain and brokenness; it's about celebrating our redemption through the blood of Jesus Christ.

But in this life, following Jesus also has costs. Costs that are sometimes seeker-insensitive. This is a faith, after all, centered upon a symbol of the most torturous and degrading of deaths: the Roman cross. This is a faith literally built on humiliation. These were realities that were hard for Jesus's earliest disciples to accept. They couldn't believe that the Messiah came to die, and in such an embarrassing way. But he did, and humility of the most extreme sort has been a hallmark of Christianity ever since. This is a path of losing life to gain it (John 12:25), putting others first

(Phil. 2:3–4), and following Christ's example of "becoming obedient to the point of death, even death on a cross" (Phil. 2:8).

To be a disciple of Jesus is to deny oneself (Matt. 16:24), to take up a cross (Luke 14:27), to be subject to persecution (John 15:20; 2 Tim. 3:12). It is to give up the creature comforts of home (Luke 9:58), to forsake the priority of family (Luke 9:59–62; 14:26), to be willing to give up all material possessions (Matt. 19:21; Luke 14:33), to be crucified with Christ (Gal. 2:20). It is also to embrace the messiness of community, bearing with one another in love (Eph. 4:2), bearing one another's burdens (Gal. 6:2), and working for a seemingly impossible unity (Gal. 3:28).

And this is just the beginning. To be a community of Jesus followers is to trade a comfortable, me-centric existence for danger, difficulty, and discomfort of all sorts. But it's the best trade you could possibly make.

2

The Uncomfortable Cross

If anyone would come after me, let him deny himself and take up his cross and follow me.

MARK 8:34

Hide not the offense of the cross, lest you make it of none effect. The angles and corners of the gospel are its strength: to pare them off is to deprive it of power. Toning down is not the increase of strength, but the death of it.

CHARLES H. SPURGEON

There is a quaint, almost vintage quality to it now, but from the pews of the little Baptist church in Oklahoma where I grew up, "The Old Rugged Cross" was a hymn that cut deep. However treacly it may have been, George Bennard's 1913 hymn nevertheless captured in my young mind the paradoxes of my developing faith.

On a hill far away stood an old rugged cross,
The emblem of suffering and shame;
And I love that old cross where the dearest and best
For a world of lost sinners was slain.

This was a faith centered upon an "emblem of suffering and shame," and yet one that captured a love beyond what I could imagine.

O that old rugged cross, so despised by the world,
Has a wondrous attraction for me.

The attraction was inescapable, to be sure. From preschool to fifth grade, the Holy Spirit worked on me hard in those pews, calling my name, drawing me to the cross, convicting me for the shame I often felt about identifying with it. I remember leaving church on humid Oklahoma afternoons, sweaty with guilt and exhausted from the struggle between my attraction and revulsion toward that old rugged thing. It was rarely easy to sing that last verse and mean it:

To the old rugged cross I will ever be true;
Its shame and reproach gladly bear.[1]

Even as my faith took firmer root and my "wondrous attraction" to the cross strengthened, the "gladly bear" part has never been easy. And yet the shame and reproach of the cross is fundamental to the journey. To be a Christian is to accept the discomfort of a way of life inspired and empowered by a cruel, rugged old cross, a symbol of scorn and degradation.

Everything uncomfortable about Christianity begins with and returns to the cross.

The Offense of the Cross

Writing to a group of early Christians in Corinth, the apostle Paul famously said, "The word of the cross is folly to those who are perishing, but to us who are being saved it is the power of God" (1 Cor. 1:18). Christ crucified was "a stumbling block to Jews and folly to Gentiles" (v. 23), a foolish thing and a sign of weakness.

In the ancient world a cross was not something decorative to cross-stitch or wear, diamond-studded, around one's neck. It was a barbaric method of slow death. Typically reserved for the worst of criminals among despised people groups, crucifixion was used by Greeks and Romans to inflict maximum pain and humiliation on deserving criminals. That the supposed King of the Jews would be subject to such a death was beyond scandalous. Who would believe in a messiah who did not overtake Roman oppressors but rather let them ridicule and execute him in such an embarrassing way? It was foolishness.

The cross of Christ was foolishness even to those in Jesus's inner circle. Immediately after Jesus confirmed his disciples' suspicions and hopes that he was the long-awaited Messiah (Mark 8:27–30), Jesus pulled the rug out from under their feet. "The Son of Man must suffer many things and be rejected by the elders and the chief priests and the scribes and be killed, and after three days rise again," he told his disciples (v. 31). Suffering? Rejection? Death? It was so preposterous that Peter began to rebuke Jesus for even suggesting it (v. 32).

But Jesus wasn't delusional. As if the news of his own impending death wasn't shocking enough, he then threw down the discipleship gauntlet: "If anyone would come after me, let him deny himself and take up his cross and follow me. For whoever would save his life will lose it, but whoever loses his life for my sake and the gospel's will save it" (vv. 34–35).

Want to follow Jesus? Join him at the cross. Just as Jesus "suffered outside the gate" on his road to Calvary, so should we "go to him outside the camp and bear the reproach he endured" (Heb. 13:13). To be a follower of Christ is to join his journey of abandoning comfort and enduring suffering, a journey that is foolishness in the eyes of the world.

The cross remains "folly" because it undermines human logic and wisdom. We have ideas about what redemption and revolution should look like. Yet the wisdom and power of God confounds us. As John Stott notes, "The gospel of the cross will never be a popular message because it humbles the pride of our intellect and character."[2]

Just as it scandalizes by embracing humility in a world where pride reigns, the cross is also unpopular because it champions weakness in a survival-of-the-fittest world. This is why Friedrich Nietzsche rejected Christianity, "the religion of pity" which "makes suffering contagious." Paul's words in 1 Corinthians 1:27 ("God chose what is weak in the world to shame the strong") represent, for Nietzsche, the "horrible secret thoughts" behind the symbolism of "God on the cross."[3]

The apparent weakness of God on a cross is also offensive to Islam, a religion that both denies the historical fact of and need for Christ's crucifixion, finding it "inappropriate that a major prophet of God should come to such an ignominious end."[4] The cross of Christ is a major dividing point between Islam and Christianity,[5] and Muslims who convert to Christianity often face ridicule and alienation from their families. The indelible, gruesome images of twenty-one Egyptian Christians beheaded by members of the Islamic State in a 2015 video capture it well. Described in a caption as "people of the cross," these orange jumpsuit-clad martyrs are in positions of weakness: vulnerable on their knees as the knives of their captors saw at their necks. And yet as they succumb to death, they do so in faith, trusting in the victory of another victim of brutal execution.

Reflecting the truism that "to live is Christ, and to die is gain" (Phil. 1:21), these martyrs lost their lives but also gained. And so it is for all people of the cross: visible loss for invisible gain, present suffering and future glory. This is the offense of the cross. Not only that a God would subject himself to such weakness and death, but also that such perceived folly would become the pride of his followers.

The Loss (and Gain) of Taking Up Your Cross

Dying by beheading on a beach will not be a likely cost of discipleship for most Christians today. Nonetheless, more than loss of life is implied in Christ's statement that a follower must "deny himself and take up his cross," just as more than death is implied in Dietrich Bonhoeffer's famous statement that "when Christ calls a man, he bids him come and die."[6]

Indeed, there are many "deaths" involved in following Christ, however obscured they may be in today's cushy forms of Christianity. The following are five likely losses that come with truly embracing the cross of Christ.

The Loss of Being Your Own Boss

There is nothing more American than being your own boss: working up the ladder, taking charge of your life and property. It's one of the reasons why rags-to-riches gurus like Oprah or unapologetically brash titans of industry like Donald Trump prove so captivating. We are a DIY nation, self-made, unregulated, FREEDOM fries! Our mantras are "Be who you want to be," "Follow your dreams," and "Find yourself." We embrace what sociologist Robert Bellah termed "expressive individualism," a no-constraints individualism bound only by the frontiers of feeling and imagination. If you can dream it, you can be it.

But these values rub up against the gospel on the point of self-sovereignty. For as much as we want to have complete control over our lives, following Jesus requires a surrender of will. Jesus is Lord and I am not. Adam and Eve couldn't accept God's law as final or binding. And thus sin was born on earth.

Following Jesus means putting aside our own desire to be God and allowing him to reign supreme in us and for us. As John Stott says, "The essence of sin is man substituting himself for God, while the essence of salvation is God substituting himself for Man."[7] Jesus paid it all on the cross. All we have to do is repent and relinquish our autonomy, accepting that union with Christ is our only hope.

Yet this is uncomfortable in our self-reliant culture. We don't want grace that requires us to relinquish our sovereignty. We're more comfortable with what Bonhoeffer calls "cheap grace":

Cheap grace is the preaching of forgiveness without requiring repentance, baptism without church discipline, Communion without confession, absolution without personal confession. Cheap grace is grace without discipleship, grace without the cross, grace without Jesus Christ, living and incarnate.[8]

Cheap grace is grace we accept insofar as it doesn't challenge our autonomy. It is grace we withdraw on our own terms, at our own convenience. But the cross kills the me-centric bent of iChristianity, which bends the Bible to support one's views and treats God as little more than a cosmic Siri to bless and comfort on demand. We need to resist the idolatry of autonomy and the folly of personal-preference Christianity.

The Loss of Consumer Religion

Christianity is not about "your best life now." It's not about self-promotion or ambitions of greatness. It's about following Christ's example, who "came not to be served but to serve, and to give his life as a ransom for many" (Mark 10:45). Christianity is about sacrifice rather than personal gain and service rather than power. This has been a bitter pill to swallow for disciples of Christ since the earliest days, when James and John were ambitious for status and power ("Grant us to sit, one at your right hand and one at your left, in your glory," they asked Jesus in Mark 10:37). The Zebedee sons were doubtless crushed to learn that the ethos of Christ's kingdom was not glory and prestige, but washing one another's feet (John 13:14). For "whoever would be great among you must be your servant, and whoever would be first among you must be slave of all" (Mark 10:43–44).

These words are countercultural and desperately needed in today's church, where many approach Christianity with a "what can I get out of it" consumer posture. Maybe it's the family-friendly community a church offers for the parents of small children. Maybe it's the single twentysomething seeking an eligible churchgoing spouse, the aspiring musician seeking audience applause, or a pastor seeking fame and fortune in the Christian book market and conference circuit. A willingness to give up these wish-list items for the sake of Christ is part of the cost of discipleship. This means dropping our dream-church demands and simply committing to a congregational family, even if it doesn't suit us perfectly.

The perfect-fit-for-me impulse of consumerism almost always fails us. When we marry someone on the basis of how well they match up with our list of desired qualities, what happens when they (or we) inevitably change? There is neither a perfect-for-me person nor a perfect-for-me church. In relationships and in faith, it's about commitment rather than consumerism; finding ways to serve rather than desiring to be served; filling a need rather than finding a niche. This is an uncomfortable but crucial cost of following Christ.

The Loss of Pride

One of the most offensive things about the cross of Christ has always been its leveling aspect, giving "insider" access to prostitutes, tax collectors, and the pariahs of society just as much as to religious and cultural elites; to Gentiles just as much as to Jews. The wretched thief on the cross didn't and couldn't do anything "good" to save himself, but Jesus still welcomed him into his kingdom.

This is offensive. There's a gut-wrenching scene in the Korean film *Secret Sunshine* that captures the scandal of grace better than any film I've ever seen. The scene takes place in a prison, as protagonist Shin-ae (Jeon Do-yeon) goes to visit her son's murderer in prison. Shin-ae, a new convert to Christianity, wants to forgive him. Her friends tell her she doesn't have to see him face-to-face in order to forgive him. But she insists. She wants to see him in person and (truth be told) wants to witness the look on his face when she offers him the gift of forgiveness.

And yet when she sits down to confront the prisoner on the

other side of the glass, Shin-ae finds him unexpectedly happy, peaceful, even joyful. "You look better than I expected," she tells him before explaining that the peace, love, and "new life" she'd found in God had prompted her to forgive him. She's "so happy to feel God's love and grace" that she wanted to spread his love by coming to visit her son's murderer. But then the shocker: the prisoner, the killer of her son, has also come to faith in Christ.

"Since I came here, I have accepted God in my heart. The Lord has reached out to this sinner," he says.

"Is that so?" replies Shin-ae, crestfallen and shaken. "It's good you have found God," she says, very tentatively.

The convicted murderer continues: "Yes, I am so grateful. God reached out to a sinner like me. He made me kneel to repent my sins. And God has absolved me of them."

And this is where Shin-ae begins to wilt.

"God . . . has forgiven your sins?" she mutters in disbelief.

"Yes," he replies. "And I have found inner peace. . . . My repentance and absolution have brought me peace. Now I start and end each day with prayer. I always pray for you, Ms. Lee. I'll pray for you until I die."

This hits Shin-ae hard. When she leaves the prison, she collapses, overcome by the horror of an idea she had not considered: that God could beat her to the punch in forgiving her son's killer, offering this criminal the only real absolution he needed. Unfortunately, Shin-ae can't accept this seeming injustice. How can a law-abiding, good citizen like her and a convicted child-killer be on the same level in terms of God's grace? She can't take that, and abandons God because of it.

The sufficiency and availability of God's grace to *all people* is scandalous, and for many, a pill too hard to swallow. We're prideful creatures. We want to believe that "right" living warrants us better standing in God's eyes than, say, terrorists and rapists and pedophiles. We want God to reward us for being good and punish others for being bad. Our pride makes it hard for us to stomach the notion that *earning* or *deserving* are not words that exist in God's vocabulary of grace.

The Jewish religious establishment in Jesus's day was utterly offended by this idea, as are many today who trip on the "grace alone" gospel because they want to believe their efforts at righteousness count for their salvation. This is why Paul describes the cross as a "stumbling block" (1 Cor. 1:23) and an "offense" (Gal. 5:11). No rule keeping, no good deeds, no circumcision or baptism or any other *-ism* can save us. Only Christ can.

The Loss of Power, Coolness, and Cultural Respectability

Closely related to the loss of pride but deserving of its own mention is the loss of power, coolness, and cultural respectability that comes with true discipleship of Christ. For all the reasons already mentioned in this chapter, and for many more to come in this book, Christianity calls people to ways of living that are decidedly uncool, politically incorrect, and just plain weird. Unfortunately many pastors and Christian leaders find this hard to accept; they want to be culturally respectable and perfectly at home in the hallways of power and celebrity. They will compromise convictions in order to keep those White House invitations coming. They want to be relevant players in the Zeitgeist, widely admired and well-liked, front row at fashion week right next to Kanye and Kim. Don't we all!

But faithfulness to the true gospel calls us to value weakness over power and reverence over relevance. "Cool" and "Christianity" are diametrically opposed on all sorts of fronts.[9] Cool is about self-promotion and narcissism while Christianity is about selflessness and altruism. Cool is transient and obsessed with the "now"; Christianity is transcendent, mindful of eternity. Cool is elitist while Christianity is humble. Cool is cynical while Christianity is hopeful. Cool is about being the first to discover a new trend; Christianity says the last shall be first (Matt. 20:16).

Whether we like it or not, Christianity is very strange and, in the eyes of polite society, only getting stranger. As Russell Moore has pointed out, the growing marginalization of true Christianity will likely force the church to more clearly grasp and articulate the otherness of the gospel: "The church has an opportunity now to reclaim our witness, as those who confess that we are 'strangers and exiles on earth' (Heb. 11:13). That strangeness starts in what is the most important thing that differentiates us from the rest of the world: the gospel."[10]

Indeed, the most important and ultimately most offensive aspect of Christianity will continue to be the gospel of the old rugged cross. As long as it is front and center in pulpits, Christians will always be uncool. John Stott puts it bluntly in *The Cross of Christ*:

> Either we preach that human beings are rebels against God, under his just judgment and (if left to themselves) lost, and that Christ crucified who bore their sin and curse is the only available Savior. Or we emphasize human potential and human ability, with Christ brought in only to boost them, and with no necessity for the cross except to exhibit God's love and so inspire us to greater endeavor. The former is the way to be faithful, the latter the way to be popular. It is not possible to be faithful and popular simultaneously.[11]

The Loss of Health, Wealth, and Comfort

In addition to being a blow to our autonomy, individualism, pride, and cultural respectability, following after Jesus Christ often pulls us into material discomfort.

The cost of following Jesus requires an open-handedness with money and earthly possessions, for example (Matt. 6:19–21; Luke 12:33–34), a point that proves especially challenging to the wealthy (Mark 10:17–31). Discipleship might also pull us away from any sense of home or comfortable places to lay our heads at night (Luke 9:57–58). Jesus also makes it clear to his disciples that they may have to put him above family. Indeed, some of the things Jesus says about family are quite uncomfortable (e.g., Matt. 10:34–39; Luke 8:19–21; 11:27–28), especially for cultures like ancient Judaism where family is everything. N. T. Wright observes:

> Family and property, then, were not for the ancient Jew simply what they are to the modern western world. Both carried religious and cultural significance far beyond personal, let alone "individual," identity and security. Both functioned symbolically within the total Jewish worldview. To both, Jesus leveled a direct challenge: those who followed him, who were loyal to his kingdom-agenda, would have to be prepared to renounce them, god-given though they were.[12]

As if the loss of wealth, property, and family are not enough, the loss of health and life itself are also possible costs of discipleship. Physical suffering, persecution, and martyrdom have been and continue to be fixtures of the Christian experience. From Paul's flogging in Philippi (among many other sufferings: 2 Cor. 11:16–33) to Stephen's stoning, Polycarp's burning at the stake to Jim Elliot's death by spear in Ecuador, the crucified Christians in Syria and the beheaded believers in Libya, the list of Christian martyrs is long and bloody. As one contemporary writer has put it:

> There is no getting around the fact that a Christian community is one that suffers. The pioneer of our faith suffered, the main symbol of our tradition is one of agony and death, and it's no use trying to remove the cruciform marks from the hands and feet of the church. The mark of the gospel is not health and wealth, but nails and blood.[13]

But the crazy thing about Christianity is that suffering and persecution are framed not in terms of fear but flourishing. For in suffering "we directly experience the gospel, because the gospel is about suffering giving way to death and beyond death to the victory of resurrection."[14] Suffering is perhaps the most literally "uncomfortable" thing about following Jesus that nevertheless grows us, strengthening our bonds as people that suffer together, deepening our devotion to and identification with Christ. The suffering of Jesus on the cross is something we can understand, something we can return to in our own moments of pain and hopelessness. For poet Christian Wiman, the suffering of the cross is a key to his faith:

> I am a Christian because of that moment on the cross when Jesus, drinking the very dregs of human bitterness, cries out, *My God, my God, why hast thou forsaken me?* . . . The point is that he felt human destitution to its absolute degree; the point is that God is *with* us, not beyond us, in suffering.[15]

To be a Christian is to count the cost and accept all loss in exchange for the gain of new life in Christ. As Paul wrote from prison in his letter to the Philippians:

> But whatever gain I had, I counted as loss for the sake of Christ. Indeed, I count everything as loss because of the surpassing worth of knowing Christ Jesus my Lord. For his sake I have suffered the loss of all things and count them as rubbish, in order that I may gain Christ and be found in him. (Phil. 3:7–9)

The Gain

Every taking-up-our-cross loss that we endure is worth it. For Christ and for us in him, weakness, suffering, and loss are not the end of the story. They lead to victory, resurrection, and eternal gain. The beautiful hymn of Philippians 2:5–11 captures it well. The first half is a descent: Christ leaves his heavenly home, forgoing his "equality with God," emptying himself and reducing himself to the form of a servant by becoming human. Then further down: he is obedient to the point of death. And further down still: "even death on a cross" (v. 8). At this lowest point the passage pivots to ascent: God exalts Christ and gives him the name above all names. Then further up: every knee worships him in heaven and earth. Further up still: "every tongue confess[es] that Jesus Christ is Lord, to the glory of God the Father" (v. 11).

This is the trajectory of the Christian life. Like Christ, we descend to ascend. We humble ourselves, shunning our status, accepting the depths of our depravity. And then we are exalted with Christ. After suffering, glory. After the cross, resurrection. Every loss is worth the gain of Christ. As C. S. Lewis famously writes at the conclusion of *Mere Christianity*:

> Give up yourself, and you will find your real self. Lose your life and you will save it. . . . Look for yourself, and you will find in the long run only hatred, loneliness, despair, rage, ruin, and decay. But look for Christ and you will find Him, and with Him everything else thrown in.[16]

Far from a symbol of shame, the cross is a symbol of victory for those who believe. We are victorious in Jesus (1 Cor. 15:57), more than conquerors (Rom. 8:37), led by Christ in triumphal procession (2 Cor. 2:14). The cross is victory over sin and deliverance from darkness (Col. 1:13); it destroys "the one who has the power of death" (Heb. 2:14); it triumphs over and shames the rulers and authorities of this world (Col. 2:15); it sets men free from the law of sin and death (Rom. 8:2).

On the cross Jesus said, "It is finished," and it was. Uncomfortable, ugly, bloody, rugged, and shameful the cross may be. But it is sufficient. It is everything.

3

Uncomfortable Holiness

But as he who called you is holy, you also be holy in all your
conduct, since it is written, "You shall be holy, for I am holy."

1 PETER 1:15-16

Faith in God is, finally, faith in change.

CHRISTIAN WIMAN

The bar was full of people, full of smoke, full of that loud, sustained
decibel hum of alcohol-fueled chatter that makes shout-talking into
someone's ear necessary for a conversation. The music was bump-
ing, full of profanity. At one point a few people were dancing on
a table. Bursts of laughter and the occasional shattering of glass
punctuated the noise. All manner of tobacco was being smoked:
cigarettes, cigars, cigarillos, pipes. And almost everyone in the bar
had just finished a day of sessions at a major Christian conference.

I was a part of that scene, one of the evangelical revelers whose
behavior was such that no observer could have distinguished us
as believers in any holy God, in any "set apart" sense. Of course
in the moment it was fun, joyful even, and we relished blending
in with the bar crowd. But in retrospect I wish I'd contributed a
better witness, living at least part of the call to "not be conformed

to this world" (Rom. 12:2). I wish I'd been more mindful of how, even in a bar, I was called to be different, to let my light shine before others (Matt. 5:16). I came home from that conference and penned thoughts about the problematic desire for faith to "fit in" with the cool kids of the world.[1]

Like many of my Christian peers who grew up in a rather moralistic, protective, separatist evangelicalism, I fell prey to the all-too-common pendulum problem in my twenties. I attended parties (and hosted some) with Christian college students and graduates where kegs, beer pong, sake bombs, and vomiting were among the evening's amusements. I watched movies and TV shows with little filter for unsavory or explicit content. In my efforts to avoid legalism, I abused Christian liberty.[2] Because who wants to be prudish or lumped in with the hypocritical, holier-than-thou evangelicals so despised by society? No one.

But as uncomfortable as it is to embrace holiness and be noticeably *different* in the way we live in the world, it is essential for our vocation as the people of God.

Why We Hate Holiness

In today's world, *holy* is the most offensive of all four-letter words. It's far more acceptable to say, "My life is so messed up," than it is to say, "I am striving to be holy." For many, Christianity's seeming obsession with holiness is one of its most distasteful qualities.

Why is holiness so reviled? One reason is simply that the pursuit of holiness also involves the acknowledgment of sin and the necessity of repentance. These are two words that are incredibly unfashionable: *sin* and *repentance*. In addition to implying that we are not good people, the words *sin*, *repentance*, and *holiness* conjure images of nuns with paddles, deceptively sweet (but kind of creepy) church ladies, and hypocritical pastors who decry the deviant sexual ethics of liberal America while they ravenously consume pornography behind closed doors.

Hypocrisy is a huge reason why we hate holiness. We've witnessed the inconsistencies of a "moral majority" that often failed morally, and fundamentalists who railed against the evils of pop culture while they perpetuated the evils of racism and sexism. We've seen too many people use the word *holy* while simultaneously ignoring the poor, condemning the homosexual, turning away the refugee, and covering up various forms of abuse.

For some nonbelievers, the idea that Christians are called to "be perfect, as your heavenly Father is perfect" (Matt. 5:48) is naive but innocuous, so long as believers keep their holiness and sin talk to themselves. What is abhorrent is when Christian morality is felt to be imposed on others or suggested as the preferred program for human flourishing. One man's morality may be OK for him, but it's not OK to suggest it is right for another. This implies a holier-than-thou superiority, and nothing is worse than being holier than thou.

Our Wariness of "Works"

Even devout Christians can be uncomfortable with the word *holiness*. Many Protestants are skeptical of too much emphasis on sanctification, for example, lest it morph into works-merited righteousness. But the history of God's covenant relationship with his people has always been one of both God's sufficient grace and his desire for our response of obedient living. In his biblical theology of covenantal discipleship, Jonathan Lunde argues for a continuity between the old and new covenants in terms of the holy living that, though not understood to *merit* the covenantal blessings, is nevertheless expected of God's people:

> Though always established in grace, each biblical covenant also includes demands of righteousness from those who trust in [God's] faithfulness to fulfill his covenantal promises. This means that covenantal grace *never* diminishes the covenantal demand of righteousness—righteousness that flows out of

covenantal faith. As a result, faith and works of obedience will always be found in God's true covenant partners.[3]

Jesus and Paul do not dispense with the importance of holiness for God's people in the new covenant. In some cases Jesus actually calls his disciples to even higher standards than the Mosaic covenant, for example in the area of divorce (Mark 10:2–12), the expansion of the murder prohibition to also include anger (Matt. 5:21–26), or the elevation of the prohibition on adultery to also include lust (Matt. 5:27–30). But why? Jesus is not upping the expectation of righteousness to make it harder for people to enter his kingdom. No, salvation is by grace through faith, not of our own works (Eph. 2:8–9). Jesus is raising the bar because he wants his people to be noticeably different, a light in the dark world. It's difference *for the sake of mission.*

The Difference Our Difference Makes

Ever since Abraham was called by God to leave his homeland to found a new nation in an unknown land (Genesis 12), uncomfortable obedience and uncomfortable difference have been a part of what it means to be the people of God. Why? Because God is perfectly holy. "Be holy, for I am holy" (Lev. 11:45; 19:2; 20:7; 21:8). God's holiness is no joke. It's why the Israelites crossing the Jordan were instructed to stay a thousand yards or more away from the ark (Josh. 3:4); it's why Uzzah died for touching the ark (2 Sam. 6:6–7). It's why the entire book of Leviticus is devoted to holy worship (chapters 1–10) and holy living (chapters 11–27). The minutiae of holiness in the Old Testament may seem a bit bizarre to us today, but that was sort of the point. Holiness is difference. It is strange. But not for the sake of strangeness. For the sake of Yahweh.

The theme of holiness and separation is reiterated in the New Testament: "But you are a chosen race, a royal priesthood, a holy nation, a people for his own possession, that you may proclaim the excellencies of him who called you out of darkness into his marvelous light" (1 Pet. 2:9). Jesus also uses the light imagery when he says his followers are to be "the salt of the earth" and "the light of the world" (Matt. 5:13–14). As Lunde notes, "Whatever Jesus intends by the images of 'salt' and 'light,' it is clear that his followers are to be *different* from those surrounding them in the world." Salt was used in the ancient world for flavoring, for fertilizer, and as a preservative, in each case bringing something different and beneficial to the substance around it. Light also brings something different and beneficial to its surroundings (darkness).[4] Like a lamp in a dark house, our light shines for a purpose: "So that they may see your good works and give glory to your Father who is in heaven" (Matt. 5:16).

For Christians, there is a discomfort in being different, but it is for a missional purpose. It is for the sake of the world. As Rod Dreher notes in *The Benedict Option*, embracing a countercultural identity as Christians is not about our survival as much as our task to be a light to the world: "We cannot give the world what we do not have."[5]

As historians of the early church have pointed out recently, the earliest Christians recognized the vital importance of habits and behavior that were starkly different from those of the surrounding culture. For them, more important than *believing* in Christian virtues was living them, "embodying the Christian good news, bearing it in their bodies and actions, living the message visibly and forcefully so that outsiders would see what the Christians were about and, ideally, would be attracted to join them."[6]

But our pursuit of holiness is also an act of worship, a response to God's grace. The opening of Romans 12 calls Christians to "present your bodies as a living sacrifice, holy and acceptable to God, which is your spiritual worship" (v. 1). And the next verse underscores the connection between holiness and difference: "Do not be conformed to this world, but be transformed by the renewal of your mind" (v. 2).

"Do not be conformed to this world" is one of the most grating verses of the Bible to many modern ears, yet it is not just a Pauline one-off. The nonconforming set-apartness of God's people is a major theme of the whole Bible. But it's an unpopular idea these days, both for Christians who wish they could blend in and for nonbelievers pressuring religious institutions to compromise on their different-ness (for example in the recent push for Christian colleges to abandon their policies on sexual conduct, or for Christian business owners to provide services or insurance policies that compromise their beliefs).

But the logic of groups necessitates difference. In order for *any* group—whether a Jewish seminary, an African-American college fraternity, or an LGBT advocacy organization—to have a meaningful identity and flourish in its function, it must have boundaries. If a Jewish seminary started enrolling radical, Jew-hating Muslims, or if an African-American fraternity allowed white women to join, or if GLAAD hired James Dobson as its new president, these groups would cease to have any meaningful differentiation. In the same way, a Christian college or church ceases to be relevant when it abandons its conviction-driven distinctions to fit the prevailing winds of politics and culture. Pluralism only makes sense if individual groups are allowed to be themselves. When boundaries are blurred and set-apartness is lost, everyone loses.

This is why Christian difference matters. When we blend in, when our boundaries are blurred or disappear altogether, our light in the darkness fades. Our salt loses its saltiness. This is why the shift Russell Moore describes in *Onward*, from an evangelical "moral majority" to a "prophetic minority," is a good thing. It doesn't mean we disengage from culture or build impenetrable, dialogue-averse walls around our institutions. What it means is *engaged alienation*: "a Christianity that preserves the distinctiveness of our gospel while not retreating from our callings as neighbors, and friends, and citizens."[7]

The more Christians look, talk, act, and believe like the culture around us, the less interested others will be in what we have to offer. Why would anyone go to church and bother with Christianity if it is only a replica of the sorts of things they can find at the mall, movie theater, community center, or nightclub? It is the different-ness of the gospel, not its hipness, that changes lives and transforms the world.

Our "Brokenness" Obsession

One of the particularly troubling ways evangelical Christians have copied the larger culture in recent years has been their embrace of "brokenness" as the Holy Grail of authenticity.[8] The imperfection of Christians has become a point of emphasis, a badge of honor within evangelical culture. Books were published with titles like *Messy Spirituality*, *Death by Church*, and *Jesus Wants to Save Christians*, and churches popped up with names like Scum of the Earth and Salvage Yard. Evangelicals made films like *Lord, Save Us from Your Followers*, wrote blog posts with titles like "Dirty, Rotten, Messy Christians," and maintained websites like anchoredmess.com, modernreject.com, churchmarketingsucks .com, recoveringevangelical.com, and wrecked.org—a site that includes categories like "A Hot Mess," "Muddling Through," "My Broken Heart," and "My Wreckage."

Meanwhile, self-deprecating humor sites like *Stuff Christians Like* and *Stuff Christian Culture Likes* became hugely popular repositories of Christianity's many warts, and writers like Anne Lamott and Donald Miller became best-selling, "nonreligious" expositors of messy spirituality.

Erik Thoennes, professor at Biola University and elder at Grace Evangelical Free Church in La Mirada, California, sees the authenticity trend in the undergrads he teaches. At the beginning of each class he asks his students to write down two things they love and two things they hate. Consistently, one of the things they say they hate is "fake people." But the Christian life involves a whole lot of "fakin' it" on the path to becoming more like Christ, Thoennes says.

"There's this idea that to live out of conformity with how I *feel* is hypocrisy; but that's a wrong definition of hypocrisy," Thoennes says. "To live out of conformity to what I *believe* is hypocrisy. To live in conformity with what I believe, in spite of what I feel, isn't hypocrisy; it's integrity."

Thoennes hopes his students understand that sanctification involves living in a way that often conflicts with what feels authentic. Still, he gets why younger evangelicals have such a radar for phoniness. They grew up in an evangelical culture that produced more than a few noteworthy cases of fallen leaders and high-profile hypocrisy. Their cynicism reflects a church culture that often hid its imperfections beneath a facade of legalism and self-righteousness. As one young evangelical wrote for *Relevant* in 2007, "Authentic community, authentic faith, and authentic Jesus are the cry of the new generation. . . . We don't want to be fooled anymore. We don't want to be gullible anymore. . . . We want flawed. We want imperfect. We want real."[9]

But why must "real" be synonymous with flawed and imperfect? When someone opens up about their junk, we think, *You're being real*, and we can relate to them. But what about the pastor who has served faithfully for decades without any scandal, loved his wife and family, and embodied the fruit of the Spirit? Is this less real?

Often, what passes for authenticity in evangelical Christianity is actually a safe, faux-openness that establishes an environment where vulnerability is embraced, only up to a point. In church small groups we share our struggles but often only those that are "safe" in their normality. A group of guys goes around the circle and each shares about their recent struggles with lust and porn, without getting into too much detail, and everyone leaves congratulating himself for having been "vulnerable" and "authentic." But is anyone being changed?

Authenticity and vulnerability are not synonymous, notes

Nick Bogardus, pastor of Cross of Christ church in Costa Mesa, California. Authenticity is a monologue, while vulnerability is by nature a dialogue, he says. "Authenticity is a placebo; it has no benefit higher than meeting a thin psychological need. Vulnerability is an invasive procedure."[10]

In many evangelical church discipleship groups, it's almost as if our sins have become a currency of solidarity—something we pat each other on the back about as fellow authentic, broken people. But sin should always be grieved rather than celebrated, Thoennes argues.

"Brokenness is an interesting word because if it's sin, we should call it that," Thoennes says. "I only feel sorry for broken people. God's mad at sinful people."

We've become too comfortable with our sin, to the point that it's how we identify ourselves and relate to others. But shouldn't we find connection over Christ, rather than over our depravity? By focusing on brokenness as proof of our "realness," have we made authenticity a higher calling than holiness?

Holiness Is More Authentic Than Brokenness

Our notion of authenticity should not primarily be about affirming each other in our struggles—patting each other on the back as we share about porn struggles while enjoying a second round of beers at the local pub Bible study. Rather, authenticity comes when we collectively push each other, by grace, in the direction of Christlikeness.

Reflecting on Christians' "current obsession with brokenness," Megan Hill writes, "If we are constantly looking for someone else who is broken in all the same places, we overlook the comfort we can have in the perfect God-man. . . . Grace covers. And it covers again and again. Thanks be to God." But if we stop there, "we are only telling half of the story. . . . Receiving grace for my failures also includes Christ's help to turn from sin and embrace new obedience."[11]

Could it be that the most authentic thing any of us can do is faithfully pursue holiness and obediently follow after Christ? In Scripture, Paul teaches again and again that Christians are "dead to sin" and risen to new life, no longer slave to sins but to righteousness (Romans 6). That doesn't mean the battle with sin is gone. But as Paul describes the struggle in Romans 7, he says, "It is no longer I myself who do it, but it is sin that dwells in me" (Rom. 7:17), noticeably separating his identity from this unwanted, alien thing still residing within. The struggle is neither the point nor the marker of one's identity. In Christ we are new creations (2 Cor. 5:17), called to flourish through life in the Spirit (Romans 8).

"I think goodness is more real in that we are actually living more as humans were intended to," Thoennes says. "Jesus is the realest human we'll ever see. He's authentic. He understands our brokenness. But he's as real as can be."

To overcome our authenticity confusion, evangelicals must see themselves differently. Rather than focusing on our brokenness, we should look to Christ and those who model Christlikeness. We should move in that direction, by grace and through the power of the Holy Spirit. We should also, perhaps, stop speaking of ourselves in such "we are scum" terms. In Christ we can be more than scum. And that's a message the world sorely needs.

Hard as it may be to believe in the midst of our sinful thoughts and fleshly struggles, we were made to be perfect. Brokenness may feel more natural, but holiness is actually the more human state. Our image-of-God wiring is for Christlikeness, not devil-likeness. As Scott Sauls writes, "To err isn't human after all. To err is, cosmically speaking, an anomaly. That's why we can't bear the imperfection in ourselves and in others."[12] C. S. Lewis puts it this way: "The more we get what we now call 'ourselves' out of the way and let Him take us over, the more truly ourselves we become."[13]

The Christian life is not a call to be true to yourself. It's a call to deny yourself, or at least to deny those parts of yourself that are incompatible with the human type we should all aspire to imitate: Jesus Christ. As Stott says, "True self-denial (the denial of our false, fallen self) is not the road to self-destruction but the road to self-discovery."[14]

We love talking about how Jesus "meets us where we are at," and it is true that he does. But he doesn't want us to stay where we are. Insofar as "authenticity" keeps us in our muck and inhibits growth toward holiness, then authenticity is an enemy of the gospel. And it is also an enemy of hope. As Bogardus notes, "If this is 'just who I am,' then what hope is there for me for change? What hope is there for something better? God, save us from mere authenticity."[15]

Change We Can Believe In

The Christian life is a life of change: always growing and always pursuing righteousness as new creations of God. If we are not a people compelled by the sanctifying, shaping power of the Holy Spirit to change us from who we are to who we are meant to be, then we are not the church Jesus wants us to be.

We must believe in change. Not in the political sense, as in Barack Obama's 2008 election campaign slogan, but in the personal, moral, crucified-with-Christ sense. And this is certainly unpopular in a world far more comfortable with a "this is just who I am" justification of sin.

As fallen beings we are all naturally full of disordered desires, misshapen longings, proclivities, and addictions we wish we didn't have. But what we don't need in this state are people who affirm us in our brokenness and urge us to continue "being who we are."

A few years after graduating from college, I went to a New Year's Eve party in downtown Chicago and got knock-down drunk (the only time in my life thus far, thankfully). It was so bad that I only vaguely remember that my best friend had to hold my head over the toilet a few times and then later help me change shirts (I had vomited chili all over my sweater). It was ugly. The next day my friend, who had so graciously been there for me in the ugliness of my drunkenness, told me how disappointed he was in me and how embarrassed he was on my behalf. It was hard for me to hear, but I'm so glad he said it. I'm so glad he didn't laugh it off or say, "Happens to us all, man." I'm glad he called it what it was: sin. The physical hangover was one thing; the shame of my sin is what motivated me to strive to never do it again.

We all struggle with sin and the desires of the flesh, and sometimes it's like Dr. Jekyll and Mr. Hyde. But we must remember that "my true self is what I am by creation, which Christ came to redeem, and by calling. My false self is what I am by the Fall, which Christ came to destroy."[16]

And destroy it he did.

This is our hope for change. It is Jesus's representative work for us on the cross that frees us from toxic cycles and empowers us to faithfulness. As Lunde notes, "Grace foils legalism. But grace fuels righteousness."[17] By God's grace we can be "dead to sin and alive to God in Christ Jesus" (Rom. 6:11), crucifying the flesh with its passions and desires (Gal. 5:24). But it is only by God's grace. We can't get better on our own. Holiness is a horror if it is entirely up to us. But it isn't. Thankfully, we have in the Holy Spirit an empowering advocate to help us walk in a new way (Romans 8). It is not us, but the Holy Spirit within us, that allows for change (1 Thess. 5:23; 2 Thess. 2:13). And that's a relief.

But regardless of the freeing reality that change comes not from our own strength, the call to holiness remains an unpalatable idea in today's world, as is the requirement of repentance. To believe in a change that favors self-denial over self-actualization, to suggest that holiness is more authentic than brokenness, and to assert that all of this is liberating rather than stifling . . . in the eyes of many, these are first among a long list of Christianity's uncomfortable but stubbornly essential truths.

4

Uncomfortable Truths

Jesus said to him, "I am the way, and the truth, and the life.
No one comes to the Father except through me."

JOHN 14:6

We must allow the Word of God to confront us, to disturb our
security, to undermine our complacency and to overthrow our
patterns of thought and behavior.

JOHN STOTT

Some who might otherwise find Jesus appealing are turned off by
Christianity as a system of beliefs because some of those beliefs are
just too hard to stomach. There are some parts of the Bible that,
frankly, we might wish weren't there.

The purpose of this chapter is not to provide an exhaustive list
of all such "uncomfortable truths," nor is it to wrestle substan-
tively or sufficiently with the nuanced questions associated with
them. Rather, I want to give a sampling of some of the biblical
truths that have been and continue to be stumbling blocks for people both inside and outside of Christianity. I'll be discussing three
groupings of truth that in my experience prove most challenging to

twenty-first-century people: (1) the supernatural, (2) Christianity's exclusivity and God's wrath, and (3) sexual ethics.

Since my aim here is not to settle any of these issues as much as it is to summarize why they are uncomfortable, this chapter may (and probably should!) leave you wanting more. For that reason, at the end of this chapter I have included a short list of recommended books for each section, written by theologians and philosophers far more equipped than I am to rigorously grapple with these difficult issues while maintaining fidelity to the authority of Scripture.

The Supernatural

Let's start with a truth that is inescapable in Christianity but unavoidably far-fetched to many: the existence of the supernatural. Christianity presupposes an eternal, all-powerful God who cannot be examined under microscopes or tested by the scientific method. Christianity also assumes that this God created everything in the universe (Genesis 1–2) and can miraculously intervene in the natural order, whether in sending a massive flood (Genesis 7–8), creating dry pathways through rivers (Ex. 14:21–31; Josh. 3:14–17), or turning water at various times into blood or wine (Ex. 7:14–25; John 2:1–11).

The Bible is rife with instances of the supernatural that would seemingly be more at home in a Harry Potter novel than a religious text taken seriously by billions of twenty-first-century people. Here is just a small sampling:

- Mystery food from the sky (Ex. 16:14–35) and water from a rock (Ex. 17:5–7)
- Aaron's staff turning into a snake (Ex. 7:10–12) and later blossoming and producing almonds (Num. 17:1–11)
- Days longer than twenty-four hours because "the sun stood still" (Josh. 10:12–14)
- Three men survive standing in a blazing fire (Dan. 3:10–27)

- A man survives being swallowed by a big fish (Jonah 2:1–10)
- A man has a conversation with a talking donkey (Num. 22:21–35)
- Mary, a virgin, becomes pregnant with the Son of God (Luke 1:34–38)
- Jesus heals blind people (Matt. 9:27–31), deaf people (Mark 7:31–37), and lepers (Luke 17:11–19), to name a few
- Jesus walks on water (Matt. 14:25; Mark 6:48; John 6:19)
- Jesus turns five loaves of bread and two fish into enough food for five thousand people (Matt. 14:15–21; Mark 6:30–44; Luke 9:10–17; John 6:1–14)
- Jesus raises people from the dead (Mark 5:23–42; Luke 7:11–18; John 11:38–44)
- Jesus raises himself from the dead (Matt. 28:1–10; Mark 16:1–8; Luke 24:1–12; John 20:1–10)

The prevalence of supernatural craziness is embarrassing for many Christians. But miracles are indispensable in Christianity. Without the miracle of miracles—the resurrection—there would be no Christian faith. Old Testament instances of the supernatural might be explained away as culturally specific literature and not historical fact, but the resurrection of Jesus as described in the Gospels is a necessarily historical lynchpin.

Dispense with the supernatural and you dispense with Christianity. If there is no supernatural God, no resurrection, no Holy Spirit (more on this in chapter 6), there is nothing. As Russell Moore puts it, "The Christian message isn't burdened down by the miraculous. It's inextricably linked to it. A woman conceives. The lame walk. The blind see. A dead man is resurrected, ascends to heaven, and sends the Spirit."[1] But this is all very uncomfortable to modern people.

It wasn't always this way. The supernatural wasn't nearly as unbelievable to people in the ancient world as it is to us now.

But things have changed. As Charles Taylor illustrates in *A Secular Age*, the transition has been gradual from a Western world where it was once impossible to *not* believe in God to one where disbelief in God is widely acceptable, if not the norm. As the Middle Ages gave way to the Renaissance, the scientific revolution, and the Enlightenment, belief in God and the supernatural began to erode. Deism emerged in the seventeenth and eighteenth centuries as a sort of compromise for those who championed rationality but didn't want to get rid of religion entirely. Deist Thomas Jefferson, for example, admired the teachings of Jesus but rejected the supernatural aspects of Christianity. He made his own Bible (titled *The Life and Morals of Jesus of Nazareth*) by literally cutting and pasting the parts that he liked and disregarding anything that he saw as "contrary to reason."[2]

Jefferson's creative attempt to "save" Jesus from the miraculous seems silly to us in the twenty-first century, in part because it's far more acceptable today to just abandon theism altogether. Why go to all that trouble to cut-and-paste the moral message of Jesus if the whole Bible is built on shaky supernatural ground? We can be good without God after all, right?

Religious practice is still prevalent, of course, but the currents of naturalism are strong, especially among well-educated Westerners. Many assume intellectual respectability precludes belief in the existence of God, the soul, angels, demons, and so forth; that such things are in the same category as elves, wizards, or leprechauns. They may be "experienced" in some mystical way, but they can't be observed by science or *known* in a rationalistic sense.

And herein lies the issue behind the issue for the "supernatural" barrier of faith: it confronts human pride because it places limits on what we can know and understand. And this is uncomfortable for everyone. It's uncomfortable for materialists whose paradigms don't allow for dead people to reanimate; it's also uncomfortable for six-day creationists who refuse to accept that *we can't really know for sure* how the creation of the world played out.

Even though God gave humans reasonable minds, which can absolutely enhance our experience of him (or enable our disbelief in him!), our minds are still *limited* in their capacity to fully grasp concepts (eternity, the Trinity, the incarnation, grace) that must be believed in faith.

Christianity's Exclusivity and God's Wrath

> I am the way, and the truth, and the life. No one comes to the Father except through me. (John 14:6)

Those are among the most offensive two sentences Jesus ever spoke. In a world where multiple roads supposedly lead to heaven, a "Jesus is the only way" approach is abhorrent. It was the case in Ephesus when Paul's preaching against the goddess Artemis caused riots (Acts 19:23–41), and it is true today.

One reason Christ's exclusive claims don't sit well with us is that we don't like the implications for our friends and neighbors of other faiths, let alone people on the other side of the world who— simply by virtue of where they were born—have never heard the gospel.

Rachel Held Evans poignantly articulates the problem in describing her middle school experience of reading *The Diary of Anne Frank*. Since Anne was Jewish and had not accepted Jesus Christ as her Savior, did that mean she was burning in hell alongside Nazis? For Evans, this thought caused an early fracture in her faith:

> In Sunday school, they always make hell out to be a place for people like Hitler, not a place for his victims. But if my Sunday school teachers and college professors were right, then hell will be populated not only by people like Hitler and Stalin, Hussein and Milosevic but by the people they persecuted. If only born-again Christians go to heaven, the piles of suitcases and bags of human hair displayed at the Holocaust Museum represent thousands upon thousands of men, women, and

children suffering eternal agony at the hands of an angry God. If salvation is available only to Christians, then the gospel isn't good news at all. For most of the human race, it is terrible news.[3]

This is indeed an uncomfortable truth, for it directly confronts our senses of justice and compassion. We naturally struggle with the idea that only a select group will be inheritors of God's kingdom. Many of us have an even harder time stomaching the idea of election, that those who freely come to God are those whom God has freely chosen, an idea Tim Keller admits is "not easy to accept."

But regardless of what we think about divine election, we must all face the same hard question, says Keller: "Why wouldn't God save us all if he has the power and desire to do so?"[4]

The flip side of this question raises even more uncomfortable questions: Are the unsaved, or non-elect, really condemned to suffer the eternal judgment and wrath of God?

In a video trailer for his 2011 book *Love Wins*, Rob Bell describes a piece of art he saw featuring a Gandhi quote. Someone posted a note on the art saying: "Reality check. He's in hell." To which Bell replies in the video: "Gandhi's in hell? He is? And someone knows this for sure? . . . Will only a few select people make it to heaven, and will billions and billions of people burn forever in hell?"

Bell then describes how millions have been taught that God will send you to hell if you don't believe in Jesus, which conveys the message that Jesus rescues you from God.

"But what kind of God is that, that we would need to be rescued from this God?" asks Bell. "How could that God ever be good? How could that God ever be trusted? And how could that ever be good news?"[5]

Bell isn't the only one asking questions like these. In their arguments against religion, atheists suggest that the wrathful

God of the Bible (particularly in the Old Testament) is morally reprehensible. Richard Dawkins minces no words in describing Yahweh as

> ... arguably the most unpleasant character in all fiction: jealous and proud of it; a petty, unjust, unforgiving control-freak; a vindictive, bloodthirsty ethnic cleanser; a misogynistic, homophobic, racist, infanticidal, genocidal, filicidal, pestilential, megalomaniacal, sadomasochistic, capriciously malevolent bully.[6]

Critics like Dawkins point to passages in the Old Testament that seem to show God commanding genocide against non-Israelite ethnic groups. In Deuteronomy 20:16–18, God calls for his people to utterly destroy the Canaanites. Passages in Joshua suggest that the conquest of Jericho included the slaughter of more than just enemy soldiers ("both men and women, young and old," 6:21), as did the destruction of the city of Ai ("all who fell that day, both men and women, were 12,000, all the people of Ai," Josh. 8:25). In 1 Samuel 15, God tells Saul to utterly destroy the Amalekites, including "both man and woman, child and infant, ox and sheep, camel and donkey" (v. 3). Against the Midianites, God commands Moses to "kill every male among the little ones, and kill every woman who has known man by lying with him. But all the young girls who have not known man by lying with him keep alive for yourselves" (Num. 31:17–18).

Critics argue that these and other passages paint the picture of a fearsome, homicidal God and a Bible that provides "a warrant for trafficking in humans, for ethnic cleansing, for slavery, for bride-price, and for indiscriminate massacre."[7] Indeed, they argue, the Old Testament "holy wars" have been the inspiration for the Crusades, the Inquisition, imperialistic conquests, genocides, ethnic cleansing, and other evils throughout history.

Even conservative Christian theologians and philosophers have found the Old Testament "holy war" passages difficult. "This issue" writes Paul Copan, "is certainly the most weighty of all Old Testament ethical considerations."[8]

The discomfort caused by these passages has led many Christian thinkers to seek creative solutions. Some have suggested that the human authors exaggerated the holy war texts or attributed to God a command he didn't actually give; but this reasoning, as philosopher and apologist William Lane Craig has pointed out, may undermine biblical inerrancy.[9] Others have argued that the Old Testament's portrayal of God is too inconsistent with the New Testament's, and that the former should thus be taken with a grain of salt; but aren't these scholars simply repeating the Marcion heresy or pitting God against himself?[10]

Theologians go to great lengths to reconcile the love and wrath of God because the tension is real and unavoidable. Is God compassionate and merciful, as Jesus seems to be? Or is he bloodthirsty and hot-tempered, as he appears to be in the Old Testament passages mentioned above? Can he be both?

The issue of hell is the explosive flashpoint of this uncomfortable tension within Christianity, and Rob Bell's *Love Wins* is just one example of the interpretive gymnastics some undertake to resolve it. Yet the topic of hell and examples of God's wrath and judgment are unavoidable throughout Scripture, and not just in the Old Testament. Jesus talks about hell more than anyone in the Bible. And though we may agree with C. S. Lewis on hell that "there is no doctrine which I would more willingly remove from Christianity than this," we cannot get rid of it. "It has the full support of Scripture and, specifically, of our Lord's own words."[11] An uncomfortable truth it remains.

Sexual Ethics

What the Bible has to say about sexual ethics is perhaps the most off-putting aspect of the Christian faith in today's world. What makes a Christian sexual ethic so increasingly unpalatable is that it confronts and undermines core values in Western culture: autonomous identity, freedom, equality, authenticity. Challenging what one feels is true in the area of sexuality is to challenge one's core identity and to impose unfair restrictions on one's ability to love—or so the logic goes. To suggest that God places limits or boundaries on human sexuality *for our benefit* sounds ridiculous to many ears.

Christianity's sexual ethic is actually pretty simple, summed up by Keller as, "Sex is for use within marriage between a man and woman."[12] It's the implicit denials within this statement that prove distasteful. Like the "I am the only way" claim of Christ, the notion that sex can only look a certain way is offensive in its exclusivity.

Much has been made in the last decade of how young people are being turned away from Christianity in large part because of its "anti-gay" image.[13] Most pastors and church leaders I have talked to agree that Christianity's anti-homosexuality image is the biggest stumbling block for would-be converts. Tyler Braun, a pastor at New Harvest Church in Salem, Oregon, has said this:

> People outside of the church automatically judge that we hate gays and are therefore discriminatory toward them. The offensive part of this, to them, is how can a supposedly loving God not accept people just the way they are? Why can't people be who God made them to be? Or so they question.[14]

This issue is a particularly uncomfortable one for me. Like an increasing number of Christians in my generation, I have close friends, people whom I love dearly, who identify as gay. What does it look like for me to show love to my gay friends, even as I remain committed to the authority of Scripture on homosexuality? What does it mean that one of my gay friends is actively serving in his local church and seems to be bearing fruit for the kingdom? The questions are uncomfortable. The issue is difficult. But Scripture is unavoidable.

A biblical sexual ethic, however, goes far beyond forbidding homosexual practice. That's a truth many Christians conveniently forget. The biblical witness on sexuality is all encompassing and can be costly for all. The following are just some of the uncomfortable truths about sexuality that we must reckon with in a faithful pursuit of Christ.

10 Uncomfortable Truths about Christian Sexual Ethics

1. God created and celebrates sexual bodies and sexuality. Contrary to Gnostic, body-shaming tendencies within some strands of Christianity, the human body and its sexual functions are neither dirty nor demeaning in God's created order. As Keller says, "Biblical Christianity may be the most body-positive religion in the world."[15] God created male and female bodily differences and celebrates their goodness. He created sex as a gift and encourages it (see Prov. 5:19; 1 Cor. 7:3–5; and especially Song of Solomon). Structured as a chiasm with an orgasm at the center ("come to his garden," 4:16; "I came to my garden," 5:1), Song of Solomon is one big, beautiful celebration of heterosexual sex as a pleasurable gift. Uncomfortable truth indeed!

2. Christian sexual conduct should be noticeably different than the world's. This has been true since the earliest days of Christianity in the Roman world, where the prevailing sexual reality "was a total lack of sexual inhibition"[16] and where most people took it for granted that the goal was to have "as much sex as they could get."[17] Early Christian converts came from this context, and many of them struggled with habituating away from old sexual habits. As McKnight points out, same-sex sexual relations "was the story of more than a few of Paul's converts."[18] Yet early Christians were called to a new, different ethic of sexuality that was about something bigger than satisfying personal sexual appetites (see Romans 1; 1 Corinthians 6; Ephesians 5; etc.).

3. Sexuality is not a private matter. The Bible knows nothing of Western culture's idea that no one should tell anyone what he or she can and can't do in the privacy of his or her bedroom. Paul's position in the New Testament (see 1 Corinthians, for example) is that "everything that we do as Christians, including our sexual practices, affects the whole body of Christ."[19]

4. Sex outside of marriage is never OK. In contemporary society sex is seen as a casual thing that can be part of dating or even noncommittal one-night stands between two or more consenting adults. But God created sex for the context of the covenantal union of one man and one woman (see Gen. 2:24; Matt. 19:3–6; 1 Cor. 7:2). As tempting as it may be to see premarital sex as a way to build deeper intimacy or to "test drive" a potential mate to determine compatibility, there is simply no biblical justification for it.

5. Sexual immorality includes words and thoughts. Lest we think we are living according to God's plan simply by not having sex outside of marriage, Scripture is clear that sexual immorality includes things like lusting (Matt. 5:28), causing others to lust (see Prov. 5:1–23; 7:1–27; 1 Tim. 2:9–10), and talking luridly about sexual immorality (Eph. 5:3–4).

6. Being "born this way" doesn't excuse sexual immorality. Everyone is born with bents toward certain sins, including sexual sins. Whether this is nature or nurture, it matters not. "Just because we have that bent doesn't mean we must act upon it," says David Platt. "We live in a culture that assumes a natural explanation implies a moral obligation. If you were born with a desire, it's essential to your nature to carry it out."[20] That Scripture calls us away from this logic is very uncomfortable indeed.

7. Both the Old and New Testaments consistently forbid homosexual practice. Any time homosexuality is mentioned in the Old Testament, it is condemned (e.g., Genesis 19; Lev. 18:22; 20:13). The Torah that Jesus and Paul would have grown up studying was uniform in its disapproval of homoerotic behavior. And contrary to the assertions of some critics, "the earliest Christians did, in fact, consistently adopt the Old Testament's teaching on matters of sexual morality, including homosexual acts."[21] Though only a handful of New Testament texts (Romans 1; 1 Cor. 6:9–11; 1 Tim. 1:8–11) address homoerotic activity, "all that do mention it express unqualified disapproval," argues Duke Divinity scholar Richard Hays. The New Testament paradigm for homosexual behavior is "emphatically negative," argues Hays, and "offers no accounts of homosexual Christians, tells no stories of same-sex lovers, ventures no metaphors that place a positive construal on homosexual relations."[22]

8. Paul singles out homosexuality as an illustration of the root problem of sin. In Romans 1, Paul discusses man's rebellion against God by highlighting homosexuality as a particularly vivid example of humans rejecting God's sovereignty and refusing to honor his created order. Paul singles out homosexual intercourse in such a theological context, Hays notes, because when human beings exchange their created roles (man and woman for each other, to be fruitful and multiply) for homosexual intercourse, "they *embody* the spiritual condition of those who have 'exchanged the truth about God for a lie.'"[23]

9. Churches should value singles and the vocation of singleness. Whether for the sake of same-sex attracted Christians for whom marriage will never be an option, or for heterosexual singles who may never marry, churches must do a better job articulating a compelling vision of singleness and celibacy as callings that can be as satisfying and impactful for the kingdom as any other. Jesus, "the most fully human person who ever lived," never married.[24] Neither did Paul, who commended singleness as a worthy vocation for some (1 Cor. 7:8–9, 25–40). Churches must consider singles as "full members" of the people of God, including them in leadership teams and welcoming them at the tables and in the rhythms of church life.

10. Churches must commit to loving and walking alongside same-sex-attracted people. Heterosexual Christians must recognize and respond to the burden of their same-sex-attracted Christian brothers and sisters whose commitment to celibacy may lead them to feel hopelessly confined to a life of loneliness and suppressed libido. As Scott Sauls points out, straight Christians must do more than preach about the boundaries of "no sex outside of male-female marriage!" Rather, "we must ask the radical question of what it will take to ensure that every unmarried person has access to friendships as deep and lasting as marriage and as meaningful as sex."[25] A community like that may be awkward and messy and, yes, uncomfortable, but it beautifully pictures Christ's sacrificial love.

———

It is appropriate that we end this rather difficult chapter on the importance of sacrificial love in community. For it is precisely the radical love of Christ that will help us navigate the challenges that arise from the uncomfortable truths we've just surveyed. These are difficult questions and topics, to be sure, and every believer in today's world must grapple with them and be prepared to offer answers to skeptical challenges. But even if doubts remain on these matters for believers, God's grace remains sure. As my pastor, Alan, likes to say, "The gospel does not depend on our 100 percent certainty, but on Jesus's 100 percent sufficiency." It is God's uncomfortably persistent, sacrificial love, even "while we were still sinners" (Rom. 5:8), that is our secure foundation as we strain after certainty. And it is to that uncomfortable love that we now turn.

Further Reading

On the Supernatural

William Lane Craig, *Reasonable Faith: Christian Truth and Apologetics*, 3rd edition (Crossway, 2008).

John C. Lennox, *God's Undertaker: Has Science Buried God?* (Lion Hudson, 2009).

C. S. Lewis, *Miracles: A Preliminary Study* (Collins/Fontana, 1947).

Alvin Plantinga, *Where the Conflict Really Lies: Science, Religion, and Naturalism* (Oxford University Press, 2011).

On Christianity's Exclusivity and God's Wrath

Joshua Ryan Butler, *The Skeletons in God's Closet: The Mercy of Hell, the Surprise of Judgment, the Hope of a Holy War* (Thomas Nelson, 2014).

Paul Copan, *Is God a Moral Monster? Making Sense of the Old Testament God* (Baker, 2011).

Paul Copan and Matthew Flannagan, *Did God Really Command Genocide? Coming to Terms with the Justice of God* (Baker, 2014).

Christopher Wright, *The God I Don't Understand: Reflections on Tough Questions of Faith* (Zondervan, 2008).

Ravi Zacharias, *Jesus among Other Gods: The Absolute Claims of the Christian Message* (Thomas Nelson, 2000).

On Sexual Ethics

Sam Allberry, *Is God Anti-Gay? And Other Questions about Homosexuality, the Bible and Same Sex Attraction* (The Good Book Company, 2013).

Kevin DeYoung, *What Does the Bible Really Teach about Homosexuality?* (Crossway, 2015).

S. Donald Fortson and Rollin Grams, *Unchanging Witness: The Consistent Christian Teaching on Homosexuality in Scripture and Tradition* (B&H Academic, 2016).

Richard B. Hays, *The Moral Vision of the New Testament: A Contemporary Introduction to New Testament Ethics* (HarperOne, 1996).

Wesley Hill, *Washed and Waiting: Reflections on Christian Faithfulness and Homosexuality* (Zondervan, 2010).

Sean McDowell and John Stonestreet, *Same-Sex Marriage: A Thoughtful Approach to God's Design for Marriage* (Baker, 2014).

5

Uncomfortable Love

Greater love has no one than this, that someone lay down his life for his friends.

JOHN 15:13

The Test of Love—is Death.

EMILY DICKINSON

I had a lot of freedom in my single days. Decisions on how to spend my time and my money were completely my own. If I wanted to spend Saturday morning writing at Goldfish Cafe in La Jolla, I could. If I wanted to donate to a charity or political candidate, or pay for a round of drinks with my friends at a pub, I could. No one stopped me when I decided to go explore China on my own. No one demanded my time on weeknights and weekends, so I often spent long hours writing, working on books and blog posts as ideas came.

Much of this changed when I started dating Kira, and especially when we got married. How I spent my time and money suddenly mattered to another person. And honestly, it was a hard transition. In our engagement I worried that marriage would reduce the time I could spend reading and writing. I feared I could no longer watch every movie or TV show I wanted to watch, nor fly to Europe on a whim if I wanted to. I suspected my blogging frequency would take a hit.

On all of these points, I was right. Marriage has meant sacrifice. I can no longer spend the entirety of my Saturdays writing in the coffee shop of my choice. Kira wants to go on walks or spend time in the sun. Not ideal for a fair-skinned Scot like me, but it's what makes her happy. Marriage is about putting the other first. It's about sacrifice, the meaning of love. The cross.

Love found its ultimate expression in Jesus Christ, who sacrificed everything for our sake. He traded his perfect heavenly home for the fragile human form. He endured shame, ridicule, torture, and death in our place. Why? Because God so *loved* the world (John 3:16) that he sent his Son, who loved us and gave himself for us (Gal. 2:20). "Greater love has no one than this, that someone lay down his life for his friends," said Jesus (John 15:3), both describing his own action and challenging his followers to follow suit.

Self-effacing and others-serving. Sacrificial. This is the central idea of Christian love. "By this we know love, that [Jesus Christ] laid down his life for us, and we ought to lay down our lives for the brothers" (1 John 3:16).

This is the uncomfortable meaning of love. It doesn't lead to easier or sexier lives. It leads to sacrifice. That's the core idea, but it applies in different ways. The following are four facets of the uncomfortable, countercultural, self-giving love that Christ perfectly embodied and that his followers should strive after.

Love Isn't a Feeling. It's a Commitment.

Love is a touchy-feely word in today's world. It's about stomachs with butterflies and cheeks that blush. It's about passion, pain, highs, lows, subject to come and go as circumstances morph. It's a *feeling* as dynamic as the weather. But if there's one thing the God of the Bible demonstrates about love, it is that it is *not* primarily a feeling. It's a commitment.

In the Old Testament, God *chose* Israel as his people, and continually chose them, even when they didn't choose him. He established a covenant with them and was a faithful Bridegroom, even when they were an unfaithful bride. Time and time again in the Old Testament, Israel is described as idolatrous and adulterous, choosing to worship idols instead of God (e.g., the golden calf in Exodus 32) and acting like a prostitute who "receives strangers instead of her husband" (Ezek. 16:32). And yet God still pursues his people. His love is steadfast. The prophetic message of Hosea captures the dynamic vividly. Played out in a real-life marital drama between Hosea and Gomer, the message of Hosea is that even when Israel is adulterous (symbolized by Gomer), the Lord (symbolized by Hosea) is faithful.

If God is our model, then love is clearly "not primarily emotion or affection, but rather a covenant *commitment* to another person," writes Scot McKnight. "Commitment does not deny emotions; commitment reorders emotions."[1]

This is not how contemporary Western culture conceives of love. The saying goes "First comes love, *then* comes marriage . . . " We see love as the emotional prerequisite for relational commitment, not the obedient outgrowth of it. Marriage is viewed as a ceremonial officializing of an already-existing state, a champagne-popping party that pays little heed to the sober vows ("for better or worse, till death do us part") that have become little more than trite phrases for romantic-comedy movie posters and bridal magazines.

Society's conflation of love and emotion has led to unhealthy expectations. We assume there must be immediate fireworks with a potential mate, for example. We buy in to Hollywood's ideas of love-at-first-sight, "soul mates," and finding *the one* who "completes me." In our work with young adults, my wife and I have seen how much of a burden these ideas can be. If there is only one out there who is THE one for each of us, how much pressure is that? Young people become obsessed with compatibility, and relationships never get off the ground because there are too many fears about being the perfect fit for one another. But *the one* is as unbiblical as it is illogical. What are the odds that the ONE woman in the world for me just so happened to work a few cubicles over from me in the administrative offices of Biola University? As my pastor Alan says, we don't marry soul mates. We marry "suitable strangers."

Society today dislikes the idea that love is *learned* as a *result* of commitment. The notion that a relationship's longevity depends not on emotional vitality but on unflinching commitment is distasteful to us. This is why many (sadly, including most Christian churches) see nothing wrong with divorce. If love is emotion, then it can come and go as emotions do. If marriage is just about us feeling happy, then the minute a marriage stops delivering happiness, it is easy to justify ending it.

Richard Hays wisely observes that the church's permissive attitude toward divorce "has developed within a wider cultural context that regards marriage as a purely private affair, based on the feelings of romantic love. One 'falls in love' and gets married; when the feeling of being 'in love' dissipates, so does the basis for the marriage."[2]

Critics are right to point out the hypocrisy of evangelicals who cling to the Bible's teaching on homosexuality but conveniently ignore its teachings on divorce. As one recent observer wrote, lax attitudes toward divorce demonstrate how "evangelical leaders appear increasingly comfortable jettisoning those parts of the Bible that might interfere with their ministry to contemporary America."[3]

If Scripture's clear prohibition of homosexual conduct is an uncomfortable truth for progressive churches, Scripture's clear teachings on divorce (Mark 10:1–12) should be an equally uncomfortable truth for many congregations with high divorce rates.

The uncomfortable principle at the core of both issues is that love requires sacrificing the sovereignty of our feelings. Love cannot survive on the basis of emotional satisfaction. It is *covenantal.* And this is a hard truth to stomach, because it requires faithfulness even when we're not feeling it, even when our "heart isn't in it."

This doesn't just apply to marriage. It's also true for the way we love our friends, our parents, our children, our neighbors. A single young man might feel restless in his present community and be tempted to abandon it for a new job or opportunity across the country, but for the sake of a commitment-based love for his friends, he stays. A teenage girl might feel frustrated by her parents and tempted to break the rules they've established, but her commitment-based love leads her to honor them instead. A mom might dream of saving money to launch a business, but her commitment-based love leads her to instead use that money to pay for her son's college tuition. A volunteer after-school tutor might grow weary with a student's lack of progress and be tempted to quit, but his commitment-based love leads him to keep working with the student.

Cruciform love doesn't always feel rewarding and it doesn't always look like progress. But it does look like sacrifice and servanthood. Which is to say, it looks like Jesus (Mark 10:42–45; John 13:1–17).

Love Doesn't Serve the Self. It Serves the Other.

Cruciform love does not insist on its own way. It is patient, it bears all things, endures all things (1 Corinthians 13). Note that this doesn't mean hating yourself or enduring abuse. It doesn't mean serving *only* others while you wither in loneliness and bitterness. Love is mutual, and relationships where only one party sacrifices are unsustainable.

But love at its best only works when each party gives more than each takes, seeking the other's flourishing *first*. This may look like weakness to the world, and Lewis is right that "to love at all is to be vulnerable,"[4] but as we've already seen in this book, weakness is strength in the economy of Christ. It's vulnerable for foster families to love a child who will only be in their care for a temporary time. It's vulnerable to speak up to a friend about a damaging pattern you observe in their life. It's vulnerable to enter a potentially dangerous situation in order to help someone at risk. This sort of love is countercultural in a world of consumerism and self-preservation, where the default is to seek first what is easiest and best for me.

One way we can embody the radical nature of this other-serving, vulnerable love is by truly being present and all in with our love. This goes for how we love God, with "an undivided heart" (Ps. 86:11 NIV), and how we love others, with our undivided attention. This means we love by being undistracted, by turning off our phones when having coffee with someone. It means we exercise humility by being good listeners, quicker to hear and slower to speak (Heb. 1:19). It might mean being inconvenienced for the sake of prioritizing physical presence: taking time out of a busy schedule to have a meal with someone rather than settling for a text message or Facebook exchange. It will likely look like uncomfortable hospitality: inviting strangers and hard-to-love neighbors into your home, or including the awkward outsider on your party invite list and then giving them the seat of honor.

This sort of self-giving love works because it is how God-in-three-persons functions. The other-serving love between Father, Son, and Holy Spirit is one in which each "magnifies the other, wants the other to have the glory, and wherever possible gives to the other."[5]

This is also how love in marriage should work. Ephesians 5 is clear that in their complementary differences and selfless postures toward the other, husbands and wives are meant to represent Christ and the church. "This mystery is profound," says Paul (5:32).

What does married love as a metaphor for Christ and the church mean for us? It means that husbands especially have an uncomfortable responsibility. In the way a husband loves his wife, he is representing Christ! Too often we represent him poorly because we fall in step with the culture's posture of self-serving, pride-building, pleasure-seeking love. Yet we are called to sacrifice for our wives as Christ sacrificed for the church.

The "mystery" is countercultural because it situates marriage as a signpost of something beyond the couple, something more important than the individuals. This is the opposite of the popular conception, which sees marriage as largely "a means of self-fulfillment accompanied by sexual satisfaction," according to David Platt:

> A man or woman's aim is to find a mate who completes him or her. In this view, marriage is an end in itself, and sexual consummation is a celebration of such completion. Yet the Bible teaches that God created marriage not as an end but as a means to an end. . . . [Marriage] is a living portrait drawn by a Divine Painter who wants the world to know that he loves his people so much that he has sent his Son to die for their sins.[6]

This is all very counter to the self-focused, "just the two of us" view of love and marriage that "suffuses almost all of our cultural narratives," observes James K. A. Smith.[7] The extravagant spectacles of today's typical wedding, "in which we get to be centre stage, display our love, and invite others into our romance in a way they'll never forget," is case-in-point, says Smith. These Pinterest-perfect parties often set up marriages to fail because they frame them as "privatized enclaves for romance" removed from a higher goal or common good. "When lovers are staring into one another's eyes," argues Smith, "their backs are to the world."

Yet love was never meant to be a hideaway experience. When it is, it invariably fails. When love is outward focused, with a mission beyond itself, it flourishes. Kira and I have seen this in our own marriage. We eschewed the "nesting" mentality of newlywed life as a "privatized enclave of romance." We opted instead to jump right into the ministry of hospitality, inviting other couples, singles, and college students into our home on an almost open-door basis. We knew from our combined giftings that hospitality was likely one of God's purposes for our marriage, and that has proven to be the case.

Little has done more to strengthen our marriage than this outward-mindedness. It has been taxing and uncomfortable at times, yes. For introverts like us it's easier to hunker down and live quietly in our own private space. But we know our marriage isn't for us. We know it will not last into eternity. But we also know it will help prepare us for that day, and hopefully others too.

Love Isn't Always Nice. It Pushes Us toward Holiness.
One of the uncomfortable things about Christian love is that it isn't always nice. It doesn't always look like tolerance. On the contrary, love is sometimes about discipline and speaking truth, even when it hurts. This again is about sacrifice—the sacrifice of potentially offending someone you care about. But even if it is met with shame or discomfort, this sort of love is undeniably loving, for it has the person's best interests in mind. As Josef Pieper puts it, "Love is not synonymous with undifferentiated approval of everything the beloved person thinks and does in real life. . . . Love is also not synonymous with the wish for the beloved to feel good always."[8]

Love hurts. It hurts because it doesn't sit idly by while the beloved destroys herself. Like Christ with the woman caught in adultery in John 8, we can lead with empathy and love ("Let him who is without sin among you be the first to throw a stone at her," 8:7) but also call a person to stop sinning ("Go, and from now on sin no more," 8:11).

Society tells us love means accepting others "just as they are," without asking them to change. But biblical love is not about solidarity in brokenness; it's about committing to each other's holiness (as well as our own).

Relationships that model this are modeling the very heart of

God, whose covenantal love for his people is grounded in discipline
and demands of righteousness. There is no contradiction between
truth and love, mercy and judgment, grace and discipline in God's
character. As David Wells puts it: "He is the source of all that is
utterly good, and such is his holy nature that he will, in judgment,
consume all that has reared itself against him and against what is
good. He both judges and is loving simultaneously."[9]

Sadly, the church often favors one end of the spectrum or the
other. Focusing on God's love without his holiness results in "a
Christianity that is benign, culturally at home, racy, politically
correct, and endlessly tolerant," argues Wells, while on the other
extreme "God's love gets eclipsed in practice by his holiness,
and then his holiness gets reduced to the accountant's old ledger
book."[10]

We need to hold the tension of truth and love. They are not
mutually exclusive. I like how Biola University president Barry
Corey talks about it in his book *Love Kindness*, as the tension
between "firm centers and soft edges."[11] Compassion does not
mean we give up our convictions, and holding firm to truth does
not mean we live without love.

The church needs to model this better. We need to take cues
from Paul, whose letters to problematic early churches (Corinth,
for example) were filled with rebuke and discipline inspired by
and grounded in profound love. Describing a painful letter he had
written to the church in Corinth, which had struggled with sexual
immorality, Paul says: "I wrote you out of great distress and an-
guish of heart and with many tears, not to grieve you but to let you
know the depth of my love for you" (2 Cor. 2:4 NIV). Whether the
people we love are unrepentant in their sin or "not acting in line
with the truth of the gospel" (Gal. 2:14 NIV), we owe it to them
to confront them, compassionately and not hypocritically (Matt.
7:4–5). As Joshua Ryan Butler puts it, "Our world is desperately
in need of love that is more than *comfort*; we need love that is also
a *confrontation*."[12]

This sort of love is risky and uncomfortable, to be sure. But it is necessary. To love someone as Christ loves is to meet them in their sin but to not let them stay there. It is to walk with them in their battles and struggles, urging them onward (and they you) in the renovation of the heart. This will be messy and painful at times, requiring grace and sacrifice on all sides. But the more love takes on a cruciform shape, the more powerful it becomes.

Love Isn't Only for the Lovable. It's for Our Enemies Too.

God doesn't love us because we are lovable, or because we first loved him. He loves us even while we rebelliously undermine his rule and flee his righteousness.

Nor did God love and choose Israel because they added something valuable to his existence or because they were irresistible. "No explanation of his love for them could be given, except his love for them," says John Stott.[13] God's love doesn't wait for us to be deserving of it. It *descends* to us, writes Wells. "We could not make our way up to him, so he made his way down to us."[14]

What does this mean for the cruciform call of Christian love? It means we don't love to *get anything*; we love to be obedient, because he first loved us (1 John 4:19). Love is not about earning, but it does require effort. Love calls us to action, to serve our neighbor (Mark 12:31), to wash our friends' feet (John 13:1–7), to hang out with sinners (Luke 5:27–32). Love *does*. And this is costly.

One of the costliest requirements of Christlike love is Jesus's call to "love your enemies and pray for those who persecute you" (Matt. 5:44). What does this look like for Christians in today's world?

Perhaps it looks like Nadine Collier, whose mother, Ethel, was one of nine victims in the 2015 church massacre at Mother Emanuel AME Church in Charleston, South Carolina. Given the chance to address her mother's killer, Collier choked back tears as she forgave him: "You took something very precious away from me.

I will never get to talk to her ever again—but I forgive you, and have mercy on your soul. . . . If God forgives you, I forgive you."[15]

Maybe it looks like loving people even if it potentially brings us harm. In 2015–2017, there was much dialogue about whether or not Western countries should admit refugees from the Middle East. Could terrorists disguise themselves as refugees and infiltrate target nations within the "Trojan horse" of the massive flood of refugees? Fears like this led to Donald Trump's infamous call to ban Muslims from entering the United States. But which reflects the character of Christ more: refusing to take in a Syrian refugee because we are concerned at the *possibility* that we could be harmed by such charity, or taking in the Syrian refugee out of sacrificial love that says, "You are welcome at my table *even if* it costs me something"?

Cruciform love is welcoming the immigrant simply because they bear the image of God, even if the only thing they bring to us is hassle and possible harm. Cruciform love is praying for those who persecute us, whether it be ISIS terrorists or political foes. Cruciform love is serving and protecting our gay and lesbian neighbors, combating racism and hateful speech of all sorts, and advocating for the image-of-God dignity of every human being. It is embracing the homeless person despite the smell, healing the wounds of a soldier even if he is unjustly arresting us (Luke 22:51), and loving those we disagree with, even if they don't love us back.

Cruciform love means clothing the naked, feeding the hungry, welcoming the stranger, and ministering to the sick, the imprisoned, and the "least of these." Cruciform love is the church financially supporting one another (1 Cor. 16:1–4; 2 Corinthians 8–9; Gal. 2:10), even if it is costly. C. S. Lewis says we should give financially to the point that it means going without some comforts and luxuries: "I am afraid the only safe rule is to give more than we can spare. . . . There ought to be things we should like to do and cannot do because our charities expenditure excludes them."[16]

Love that is only convenient and conditional is not love. To love is to go out of your way, to be inconvenienced (like the Good Samaritan), to sacrifice for the sake of another.

Early Christians were characterized by this sort of love. They were known both for their love for one another and for their pagan neighbors. As one pagan emperor of Rome observed, it was Christians' "benevolence to strangers" and the fact that "the impious Galileans support not only their own poor, but ours as well,"[17] that explained the rise of Christianity.

May that be true in our generation as well. May our radical, sacrificial, stranger-focused love fan the flames of mission. May they "know we are Christians by our love,"[18] as the song goes, not because we are great but because the Holy Spirit is at work within us. May it be as undeniable to the world as it is uncomfortable for us.

6

Uncomfortable Comforter

And I will pray the Father, and he shall give you another Comforter, that he may be with you for ever.

JOHN 14:16 ASV

Why would we need to experience the Comforter if our lives are already comfortable?

FRANCIS CHAN

Of all the Sundays for them to visit our new church, why did it have to be this one?

That was the thought running through my head one Sunday morning as Kira and I sat next to my mom and my sister, who were visiting from Kansas and attending Southlands for the first time. There were already many things about our church that I knew would be uncomfortable for them: the loud rock worship songs the congregation sings standing for thirty-plus minutes straight; the casual attire and warehouse-style architecture; the get-up-from-your-seat communion. All very different from their Southern Baptist church back home. But by far the most uncomfortable thing about the service was the "charismatic" stuff, the uncomfortable manifestations of the Comforter (John 14:16, the *parakletos*).

Southlands is a rare church that tries to balance Word and Spirit, "reform" and "revival." This was and is one of the things we love about it. But it's also quite stretching, as both Kira and I grew up in churches that were functionally cessationist. I identify with the background of theologian Sam Storms, who in his cessationist days was embarrassed by the flamboyant behavior of charismatics, especially their "flippant disregard for theological precision and their excessive displays of emotional exuberance."[1]

My journey at Southlands has helped me move beyond such stereotypes, recognizing that there are as many types of charismatics as there are Calvinists, and they're not all weird. Still, my skepticism flares up from time to time. The unpredictable nature of Southlands worship services (prophetic words from congregants, impromptu and extended times of prayer, etc.) regularly makes for awkward moments, but this Sunday was especially so. It just so happened to be the first Sunday in our nine months of attending the church that a few people spoke in tongues during a time of corporate prayer. And it was the Sunday my charismatic-skeptical family was in town. The post-church conversations with my mom and sister were challenging, as I had to defend the biblical case for things that I wasn't even sure I agreed with myself.

Especially in a Western, rationalistic culture, the supernatural activity of the Trinity's third person is weird and off-putting. But I'm beginning to see, and I challenge you to see too, that the unpredictable and often-uncomfortable work of the Comforter need not be feared or avoided. Quite the contrary.

Who Is the Holy Spirit?

Part of the reason the Holy Spirit is so intimidating is that very little is taught about him in churches. But the Bible has a lot to say about the Spirit:

The Spirit is a person. He's a full member of the Trinity, along with the Father and Son, who resides in the people of God, the church (1 Cor. 3:16; 6:19–20; 2 Cor. 6:16; Eph. 2:22).

The Spirit is our divine Comforter in Christ's absence. Jesus begins hinting at the Spirit (e.g., John 7:37–39) as the cross looms. On the night before his crucifixion, Jesus tells his disciples that the Father "will give you another Helper [Advocate/Counselor/Comforter], to be with you forever" (John 14:16). He tells them: "I will not leave you as orphans; I will come to you. Yet a little while and the world will see me no more, but you will see me" (14:18–19). The disciples might have preferred Jesus remain *physically* with them as a flesh-and-blood "*Paraclete.*" But it was the *Spirit* of Jesus Christ (Phil. 1:19) who would be their Comforter (and ours) instead.

The Spirit is not just a New Testament phenomenon. In the Old Testament, the Spirit empowered specific people at specific times for specific tasks (e.g., King Saul in 1 Samuel 16:14). In contrast, the Spirit after Pentecost is characterized as a permanent, indwelling presence of every believer.

The Spirit is at work in the conversion of believers, both as "the one who initiates our faith and as the one who is received by that same faith."[2] The Spirit helps us enter the family of God and also helps us "stay in," in the sense of continually transforming us into Christlikeness.

The Spirit guides us into truth. He is the "Spirit of truth" (John 16:13) whom Jesus says "will teach you all things and bring to your remembrance all that I have said to you" (John 14:26). The Spirit inspired the writing of the Bible (2 Tim. 3:15; 2 Pet. 1:21) and helps us comprehend its truths.

The Spirit helps believers in the desire and practice of virtue. Paul is clear that our sanctification comes not from our own efforts to follow rules, but from the Spirit of God within us (e.g., Gal. 5:16–25). Truly Christian ethics are Spirit-empowered, argues Gordan Fee: "Spirit people not only *want* to please God but are *empowered* to do so."[3]

The Holy Spirit is God's presence within each believer. The Holy Spirit given to the church at Pentecost (Acts 2) is the continuation of a biblical theme of God's presence. This includes creation (Gen. 1:26–28), the garden (Gen. 3:8), the tabernacle (e.g., Ex. 40:34–38), the temple (e.g., 1 Kings 8:10–13), the prophetic hope (e.g., Ezek. 37:27), the "God with us" incarnation of Jesus (Matt. 1:23), the Word become flesh (John 1:14), Jesus's promise of eternal presence ("Behold, I am with you always," Matt. 28:20), and the new-creation promise of God once again physically dwelling with his people (Rev. 21:1–22:5). "Whatever else, the people of Israel understood themselves to be the people of the Presence, the people among whom the eternal God had chosen to dwell on earth,"[4] and it is within this context that Paul tells Christians that *they* are God's temple and that God's Spirit dwells inside them (1 Cor. 3:16).

The Spirit empowers mission and grows the church. Jesus tells his followers: "You will receive power when the Holy Spirit has come upon you, and you will be my witnesses in Jerusalem and in all Judea and Samaria, and to the end of the earth" (Acts 1:8). That promise launched in a big way with the Holy Spirit's presence at Pentecost when Jews from the diaspora were present in Jerusalem and miraculously could understand each other across language barriers. Three thousand were saved that day, and the church was launched as a Spirit-filled proclaimer and demonstrator of God's renewed presence through Christ.

The Spirit is made manifest through gifts in the gathered church. The miraculous "manifestation of the Spirit" given to each believer (1 Cor. 12:7) is especially for the *gathered community* (1 Corinthians 14) "to build us up as we live out the life of the future in the present age."[5] The manifestation of the Spirit is thus for the common good and should be evident in the public gatherings and flourishing life of the church (1 Corinthians 12; Ephesians 4–5).

Why Is the Holy Spirit Controversial?

This last aspect of the Holy Spirit's work—the supernatural spiritual gifts given to the church—has proven divisive. Cessationists assert that certain charismatic gifts of the Holy Spirit (e.g., healing, tongues, prophecy) were only for the foundational era of the church as a crucial means by which the gospel was authenticated before the canon of Scripture was completed.[6] Continuationists believe the miraculous gifts (e.g., the nine listed in 1 Cor. 12:7–10) are still available to the church today. Cessationists still believe God does miraculous things in the world, just not through human agents with supernatural "giftings."[7]

I can relate to cessationist fears about the abuse of the spiritual gifts. Isn't "hearing things from God" a justification for almost anything? And how exactly does public speaking in tongues benefit anyone?

As a Baptist kid growing up in the Midwest, I viewed charismatic Christians as basically out-of-control loons brainwashed by a cult. I remember one time when my sister came back from a church service at a Pentecostal friend's church, reporting all sorts of strange behavior: people falling over and convulsing, laughing in the Spirit, speaking in tongues, and so on. She was naturally alarmed and so was I, hoping I'd never have to be around such things.

For much of my life I have been functionally a cessationist, motivated less by theological arguments than by fear of the freak show. I relate to Storms when he says his fears were driven by "the fear of emotionalism; the fear of fanaticism; the fear of the unfamiliar . . . the fear of what might occur were I fully to relinquish control of my life and mind and emotions to the Holy Spirit."[8]

Relinquishing control is one of the most uncomfortable parts of life in the Spirit, especially in Western cultures influenced by Jeffersonian, non-supernatural rationalism; especially for left-brained logicians, theology nerds, and "I can fix anything" men who want to cognitively grasp God without letting their emotional guard down.

The challenge of the Spirit is the challenge of holding in tension the known and the unknown, the logic of the Word and the wildness of the Spirit, the headiness of doctrine and the emotion of encounter. This is an uncomfortable but essential tension in the Christian life.

The Discomfort of Word-Spirit Balance

At Southlands I have encountered something I previously had no paradigm for: a Word-centric, Reformed church that is also "Spirit-led"; a church where John Calvin is quoted alongside John Wimber; a church where forty-five minutes of expositional, gospel-centric preaching is often preceded or followed by spontaneous bursts of prayer and prophecy. Part of the church's Spirit-led DNA comes from its global orientation and emphasis on church planting and partnership in Africa and Asia—places where charismatic gifts are far more accepted and practiced throughout the church. Though Southlands has certainly not perfected the Word-Spirit balance, it has been a place where theology nerds like me are stretched to grow in the Spirit, and flag-waving (literally) charismatics are challenged to read Grudem and memorize Scripture. And that is a healthy thing.

In his 1974 essay "The Lord's Work in the Lord's Way," Francis Schaeffer wrote this:

> Often men have acted as though one has to choose between reformation and revival. Some call for reformation, others for revival, and they tend to look at each other with suspicion. But reformation and revival do not stand in contrast to one

another; in fact, both words are related to the concept of restoration. Reformation speaks of a restoration to pure doctrine, revival of a restoration in the Christian's life. Reformation speaks of a return to the teachings of Scripture, revival of a life brought into proper relationship to the Holy Spirit. The great moments in church history have come when these two restorations have occurred simultaneously. There cannot be true revival unless there has been reformation, and reformation is incomplete without revival.[9]

Schaeffer was right. Churches that will flourish in the twenty-first century will be those centered on the "dual restoration" of reformation and revival. In the midst of threats from scientism and new atheism and postmodern DIY spirituality, a strong bent toward doctrinal foundations and theological sturdiness will be essential going forward. Yet robust theology stripped of supernatural power will make no difference in the vitality of the church in the face of growing persecution and the inertia of secularism. In the face of these threats, we must rely on and pray for more of the Spirit's power.

The life we were designed for as humans, and also as the church (the body of Christ), requires both the head and the heart, knowledge and passion, structure and spontaneity, rationality and mystery, contemplated principles and enacted power. We need both freedom and order in worship services, for example, planning corporate worship well but not so rigidly that we are closed to unforeseen movements of the Spirit and unanticipated congregational contributions (e.g., 1 Cor. 14:26).

We should guard against the dual idolatries of bibliolatry[10] ("Father, Son, Holy *Scripture*") and "the idolatry of self" that can arise when subjective experiences of worship are prioritized over encountering God through Scripture.[11] We should recognize that the gospel comes in word and "is good news that has to be understood," an emphasis Reformed charismatic Terry Virgo says must never be jettisoned, "especially today when people are full of their own ideas about God and life."[12] But neither should we jettison the Spirit, whose empowering presence for the church is vital for worship, witness, unity, mission, spiritual growth, and every other function of the body.

The complementary beauty of Word-Spirit balance is fundamental not just to the DNA of the church but to our flourishing as humans. One cannot live as a cerebral thinker without the hard-to-harness emotions and energy of the body; one cannot thrive by focusing exclusively on either predictable rhythms *or* freewheeling improvisation. We need both.

Perhaps being married for the last three years has shown this to me in a deeper way. My wife is more emotionally intuitive, flexible, and spontaneous than I am. I'm more emotionally consistent, systematic, and structured than she is. Together we are stronger in our marriage, more vibrant in our witness.

You start to see corollaries to the Word-Spirit dynamic everywhere when you look. Left-brained and right-brained. Prose and poetry. Classical music and jazz. There's an existential trueness to Word-Spirit complementarity that lends it credibility, in addition to its biblical support (e.g., 1 Cor. 2:4–5; 1 Thess. 1:5).

Will Cessationism Soon Cease?

As globalization blurs lines between Western and non-Western Christianity, and as mutual skepticism between "charismatic" and "reformed" traditions ease, hardline cessationists seem to be an increasingly rare breed. As my South African pastor, Alan, says, most Christians in the world see Western Christianity's resistance to the supernatural as quite odd. They wonder: *Why would Christians prefer to only read about God in a book when they can also encounter the Author?* Indeed, as immigration continues to change the face of Europe and North America, Western churches that refuse to be open to charismatic encounters will connect with fewer and fewer of the Christian remnant.

Cessationists are beginning to admit that rationalism is not enough in the Christian life. "Evidence alone cannot bridge the gap between us and God," writes Daniel Wallace in *Who's Afraid of the Holy Spirit?*. "The Holy Spirit does not work just on the left brain."[13]

Other cessationists join Wallace in self-critique in *Who's Afraid of the Holy Spirit?*. In his chapter "The Father, the Son, and the Holy Scripture?" M. James Sawyer calls on cessationists to "reconceptualize the work of the Spirit in far broader terms than we have in the past."[14] In his concluding chapter, Wayne Grudem describes what he sees as a growing trend of "progressive cessationism" which "rightly safeguards the primacy and sufficiency and unique authority of Scripture in guiding our lives today, but that also leaves the door open for Christians to welcome the Holy Spirit to work in ways that have not been seen frequently in cessationist churches."[15]

In my own faith, I'm learning to make more room for the Holy Spirit, just as some in my church family are learning to make more room for the Word. I'm increasingly convinced that this dual restoration of Word and Spirit is a recipe for a stronger, richer, more vibrant witness for the church in our changing world.

Leaning into the Uncomfortable Comforter

What would it look like for Word-centric, Reformed-minded skeptics (as I have been) to lean in to the discomfort of the Holy Spirit?

First step: humility. Pride and passivity are often my two biggest enemies when it comes to the Spirit. Pride in the sense that I think theology and my intellect are enough; that I can be as effective as God needs me to be without messing around with the crazy charismatic stuff, thank you very much. But this pride sadly leads to passivity and lackluster desire to fully tap into the power of the Spirit who resides within us, ready to do significant things if we are willing to risk a bit of discomfort.

The Spirit requires us to admit that our rationality isn't

enough. We can't just *think* our way to spiritual growth and missional impact. We must rely on the Spirit, and that means taking seriously Paul's commands for believers to "earnestly desire" the spiritual gifts (1 Cor. 12:31), especially the gift of prophecy (14:1).

Reformed Christians have historically stressed the non-controversial "fruit of the Spirit" (Gal. 5:22–23) over the spiritual gifts, but how can we ignore Paul's admonitions in 1 Corinthians to seek these gifts (e.g., 1 Cor. 14:39: "Earnestly desire to prophesy, and do not forbid speaking in tongues")? Some cessationist leaders find ways to explain these passages away, but other Reformed heavyweights see differently.

"I want Christians today to obey those texts," said John Piper in a 2013 blog post, noting that he himself prays for the gift of prophecy "almost as often as I pray for anything, before I stand up to speak."[16] In his own ministry Piper prays for the prophetic in the sense of saying things that are "agreeable to the Scriptures, and subject to the Scripture, that are not in my manuscript or in my head as I walk into the pulpit, nor thought of ahead of time, which would come to my mind, which would pierce in an extraordinary way, so that 1 Corinthians 14:24–25 happens."

For reserved interior processors like me, the idea of offering a spontaneous prophetic contribution in a church service is intimidating. And when a Southlands congregational member takes a microphone during a worship service to share a prophetic word, I confess to often thinking cynical thoughts. Yet Southlands elders are careful to measure all prophetic contributions against Scripture (1 Thess. 5:19–22), following Virgo's suggestion that the prophet's "great burden is to bring us back to the Bible and its authority."[17] They also filter contributions through the lens of edification (1 Cor. 14:3–4) and orderliness (1 Cor. 14:26–33), often encouraging would-be prophets to sit on a prophecy until it can be clearly and concisely communicated.

I'm thankful for this abundance of caution with regard to the prophetic, as I have seen instances where it feels more like a show-offy demonstration of what is really just good intuition ("I sense God telling me you are facing a really stressful decision") or playing the odds ("The Spirit is telling me there are some here today who are really struggling with anxiety").

Yet I have also seen how edifying the prophetic can be. On a recent Sunday, an elder at Southlands encouraged congregation members to bring "psalms and hymns and spiritual songs" (Eph. 5:19) to fellow church members if the Spirit put any in our hearts. Though awkward and truly out of my comfort zone, I felt clearly that the Spirit was highlighting a certain man in the congregation and a certain portion of Psalm 84 ("For the LORD God is a sun and shield; the LORD bestows favor and honor. No good thing does he withhold from those who walk uprightly," v. 11). I went up to him and shared the verse and prayed for him. I told him the sun and shield images stood out to me, that I felt God wanted to both shine in the darkness of his life and protect him in the battles he faced. It was awkward at first, but in the end, beautiful. After the service, we talked more, and he shared that what I had said was extremely timely and resonated deeply with him.

The prophetic need not be verbose or complicated. Sometimes it's just a simple response to the Spirit's spontaneous leading to bring biblical direction, exhortation, and clarity for a specific time and situation.

More Weirdness: Healing and Tongues

I've always believed in theory that God can supernaturally heal people if he wants to, and I've prayed for this for myself and for others many times. But have I actually believed he would? Southlands encourages prayer for physical healing, often inviting those suffering from sore ankles, migraines, cancer, or anything else to be ministered to in prayer and the laying on of hands.

One Sunday morning after a sermon on healing out of Acts 3, a woman in the church asked me and another elder to pray for her and anoint her with oil. She had chronic back pain, to the point that she couldn't stand when singing worship songs, and she couldn't bend over.

I was a fairly new elder at the time and I had never anointed anyone with oil before. I asked a church staff member if there was any in the kitchen. She came back with a dixie cup full of olive oil, and I proceeded to pray for this woman while lightly touching her forehead with oil. Is that how you're supposed to anoint someone with oil? I wasn't sure.

The other elder and I prayed that God would heal her body completely, but also that she would *believe* that God could. The woman's husband prayed for her too. When it was all over, she said she didn't feel pain. But was it too early to tell? Was it a moment of ecstatic psychosomatic delusion? I didn't know.

But it stuck. The next Sunday at church, the woman shared her story of healing with the congregation, even bending down and touching her toes (something she hadn't been able to do for years). Months later, the pain was still gone and her whole demeanor had changed.

If this story sounds outlandish to you, I don't blame you. But it's real. God does answer prayers for miraculous healing. Is the success rate of healing prayer 100 percent? No. But that's not a reason to stop praying.

I believe the miraculous ministry Jesus began continues with his followers (John 14:12), but I also believe we must be careful to not expect "on demand" miracles. It's God's miraculous ability, not ours; he can work through our faith and prayers, but the timing and prerogative is his. There can be tragic consequences when an obsession with healing morphs into a "name it and claim it" health-and-wealth gospel, where unhealed sickness is attributed to lackluster faith. Such a perspective shows an anemic theology of suffering and a misunderstanding of the nature of Christ's sacrificial call.

Charismatics must recognize that while God is omnipotent, he is also the God of all comfort in times of suffering. Likewise, cessationists must recognize that retreating into theological concepts isn't always helpful amidst suffering. The fact is, Christianity is a supernatural religion based on a man who did miraculous things, rose from the dead, and ascended to heaven, leaving that same dead-raising Spirit within us. We should expect the Spirit to do remarkable things.

I'll admit that one manifestation of the Spirit I've struggled with is "tongues." It seems clear in Scripture that speaking in tongues was normal for the early church, and Paul thanks God that he speaks in tongues "more than all of you" (1 Cor. 14:18). But in my experience, tongues-speaking more often freaks people out than it builds them up (1 Cor. 14:26). Perhaps that's why Paul is so adamant to believers in Corinth (1 Corinthians 12–13) that tongues are not a mark of spiritual status and must be done by no more than three people in one setting, and always with an interpreter (1 Cor. 14:27).[18]

As much as I relate to Storms when he describes his former perception of tongues as "gibberish . . . ignorant and undignified," I also heed his word that "we must never forget that the gift of tongues was God's idea, not man's. He gave this gift to the Church no less than the gifts of teaching, mercy, exhortation, and evangelism."[19]

Do I fully understand tongues? No. But again, a willingness to grow in the Spirit includes a willingness to cede "Everything must make sense!" rationalism. The ways of the Spirit can be wacky and weird, but they build up the body in wonderful ways.

Do Not Get Drunk (with Wine)

As with anything, the charismatic gifts can be taken to extremes; "leaning in" to the Holy Spirit can lead to abuse and excess. But is that reason enough to fold your arms and be closed off to all things charismatic? *Abusus non tollit usum.* The abuse does not invalidate the proper use. Any good thing can become a bad thing when taken to excess. Just as we should not fear the goodness of wine because we can have too much of it, neither should we fear the gifts of the Spirit because they can be abused.

It's interesting that Paul positions "being filled" with the Holy Spirit as a sort of alternative to drunkenness: "And do not get drunk with wine, for that is debauchery, but be filled with the Spirit, addressing one another in psalms and hymns and spiritual songs" (Eph. 5:18–19). As Virgo notes, "There are real comparisons as well as contrasts between being full of the Holy Spirit and full of new wine," and as uncomfortable as it may be, "our church life must be sufficiently flexible to cope with the joyful exuberance that such 'drunkenness' brings."[20]

Paul was honest about the hazards that arise within the church when it comes to the Holy Spirit. He addressed various messy situations in Corinth, but he didn't tell them to stop engaging in the spiritual gifts altogether. He tells them they must be done decently and in order (1 Cor. 14:40). Here's what Martyn Lloyd-Jones, one of the great balancers of reform/revival and Word-Spirit, once said:

> Are we like the early Christians, rejoicing and praising God, filled with gladness and joy so that we amaze the world and make them think at times that we are filled with new wine? Let us avoid all excesses, let everything be done decently and in order, but above all quench not the Spirit. Rather be filled with the Spirit and give evidence that you are.[21]

As uncomfortable as it may be for us, we must not be passive toward the Holy Spirit. The strength of the body and the effectiveness of our mission depend on our openness to welcoming the Spirit's power, the unifying catalyst for the daunting task of the church.

7

Uncomfortable Mission

But you will receive power when the Holy Spirit has come upon you, and you will be my witnesses in Jerusalem and in all Judea and Samaria, and to the end of the earth.

ACTS 1:8

When will the concept of unreached peoples become intolerable to the church? What will it take to wake us up to the dearth of the gospel among the peoples of the world?

DAVID PLATT

Devoting one's life to the mission of God is not easy. For missionaries like my cousin Darcy and her husband, Craig, who spent most of the last decade raising four kids and leading a Pioneers team in China, the challenges are endless: cultural differences, team dynamics, distant relationships with friends and family back home, health concerns, the mind-numbingly uncomfortable challenge of communicating constantly in a second or third language. But one of the biggest challenges is the "two steps forward, one step back" nature of the work, which is never finished.

"People turn to Christ, and then they hit their wife," says Craig.

"Muslims profess faith, seemingly grow rapidly and then disappear, only to reappear six months later as if nothing happened."

It's hard being part of a mission that is eternally bigger than us, with our labor's fruit often invisible or impossible to quantify.

"Sometimes you just want to be able to fix it and be done and go home and watch Netflix," says Craig, who often thinks of his ex-youth pastor who went on to become an elevator repairman. "He clocks in, fixes the problem, and goes home at night. Find the problem. Fix the problem. Complete. Check."

In moments when the discomfort of the work is overwhelming, Craig and his team sometimes look at each other and just say, "Elevator repairman."

Mission is hard. It's uncomfortable. But it's also refining. It has a way of stripping away nonessentials and focusing our purpose. As Craig has told me, "Discomfort clarifies."

So far in this book we've seen that biblical Christianity is centered on an uncomfortable reality (the cross) and an uncomfortable call (holiness) involving an array of uncomfortable truths. It's a faith that calls us to a cruciform paradigm of love and asks us to rely on the power and direction of an unpredictable Spirit. But what is it all for? To what end do we endure all this discomfort?

We endure it for mission.

We endure it because God has elected his people for a purpose. Our consumerist framework may have turned Christianity into an insular country club, but this is not biblical Christianity. We are called to uncomfortable mission beyond ourselves. Like Adam and Noah and Israel before us, the people of God are to be a blessing to the whole world, shining God's light, manifesting his kingdom, drawing others into resurrection hope and Eden-like flourishing wherever we can.

This is a high and costly calling. In many ways every uncomfortable thing covered thus far in this book, and everything that follows, is about mission: dying to our dreams and comfort in order to advance the resurrection power of Christ in this world. But at the midpoint of this book, it's worth reflecting on a few of the particularly countercultural, uncomfortable aspects of the scope and cost of mission.

Mission Includes Our Holy Living

I know plenty of Christians who get far more excited about mission "out there" than they do about their own personal holiness: passionate church planters whose marriages are a mess; progressive Christians engaged in social justice but disengaged from their own spiritual vitality. But mission and morality are not two separate categories. Christopher Wright says our holiness is "as much a part of our missional identity as of our personal sanctification." If we preach a gospel of transformation, says Wright, "we need to show some evidence of what transformation looks like."[1]

One of the unfortunate tendencies of my generation of gospel-proclaiming Christians is that we've raised our beer glasses to the prospect of church planting and the excitement of "missional living" in hip neighborhoods and cross-cultural contexts. But we've failed to realize that as much as mission is a *going to* in the geographical sense (e.g., Abraham, the Great Commission, the apostles), it also involves a *going out* from worldliness, a leaving that is "spiritual, mental and attitudinal,"[2] abandoning the worldview of self interest and adopting the worldview of God's mission.

Mission involves faith and risk, but also obedience. We can't be effective church planters if we are apathetic about our own holiness. We'll have no witness in our church's trendy, gentrified neighborhood if we're more often mimicking the Pabst-guzzling drunks at the corner bar than we are telling them about redemption in Jesus.

"God's intention to bless the nations is inseparable from God's ethical demand on the people he has created to be the agent of that blessing," says Wright. "An immoral church has nothing to say to an immoral world."[3]

As unsexy as our individual ethics may sound compared to the adventures that await on the mission field, the fact is, our own wicked heart is the first frontier of any mission.

Mission Includes All of Creation

The good news of Christ's resurrection is good news for all creation, which groans for redemption (see Rom. 8:19–23). Christ reconciles *all* things (humans, animals, plants, etc.) to himself (Col. 1:20). If we are people of the resurrection, we ought not be apathetic about the flourishing of the physical world God has entrusted to us.

Sadly, too many Christians have been unconcerned with the facts of the accelerating pace of environmental degradation. How can we sing about how much we love God, but then pay such little concern to the treatment of the earth, which is the Lord's (Ps. 24:1)? The abuse of God's creation should grieve Christians and spur us to action, not for selfish reasons or tree-hugging reasons, but out of love for the Creator and obedience to his Genesis commands to take good care of the earth, his property.

Christians have an opportunity to reclaim environmental care as a uniquely gospel-centered activity. This is what Pope Francis models so well in his recent encyclical on environmental care, *Laudato Si*. His "integral ecology" challenges today's human-centered consumerism, where anything that impedes individual sovereignty, comfort, and convenience is relativized away. He notes, for example, that concern for the protection of nature is "incompatible" with the justification of abortion or indifference about human trafficking,[4] and he suggests that a healthy respect for the created world includes a respect for the complementarity of male-female gender that is part of that creation. A robust Christian ethic of creation care is not just about combating climate change or reducing carbon footprints; it is also about defending the preciousness of life, marriage, and family as good gifts of God's created order.

But this does not mean we can be apathetic about the day-to-day call of creation stewardship. I would love to see more churches, seminaries, and Christian leaders push believers to adopt attitudes (simplicity, gratitude, attentiveness to creation) and habits (reducing water consumption, using public transit, recycling, turning off unnecessary lights, etc.) consistent with a commitment to creation care as part of mission.

It may be politically unexpected and experientially uncomfortable for conservative evangelical churches to prioritize creation care as part of their ministry emphasis, but I believe it is necessary for mission. What if more Bible Belt Baptist churches started creation-care initiatives, or at least took steps to reduce waste and improve energy efficiency in their buildings? Cultural Christianity (the kind that is more influenced by politics than the Bible) may see this as a "liberal" issue, but it's undeniably a God-mandated mission issue.

Mission Requires Us to Serve and Speak

As an introvert who still has traumatic flashbacks to door-to-door evangelism from my Oklahoma Baptist childhood, I am much more comfortable with the "serve" side of mission than the side that involves talking to people about my faith.

On a college mission trip to Paris during my Wheaton College days (yes, I know: a "mission trip" to Paris??), I loved the part where we prepared and served food for an arts ministry film outreach night. Not so fun was a street evangelism activity where we were given stacks of tracts and told to hand them out to passersby in the Bellevue neighborhood, especially awkward since we were English-speaking American tourists! Put me in a soup kitchen all day, but please don't ask me to awkwardly talk to French strangers about their eternal destiny.

Yet as uncomfortable as it is for us (and for some extroverts, maybe the soup kitchen is a harder challenge), the truth is our gospel witness involves both word and deed, proclamation and

113

demonstration. We must speak and we must serve. We must embrace the God of justification but also *justice*.

Christians bent toward theological precision and gospel proclamation should recognize that the gospel also has on-the-ground implications for things like poverty, hunger, and injustices of all kinds. As David Platt reminds us, "The gospel compels Christians in a wealthy culture to action—selfless, sacrificial, costly, countercultural action—on behalf of the poor."[5]

The two-pronged word-deed nature of mission is bound to stretch us all. For the Texas Republican Christian, the call to participate in "liberal" causes like racial justice and poverty relief may be uncomfortable. For the barista in Brooklyn, the call to speak about repentance is likely more uncomfortable.

Indeed, the awkwardness of sharing your faith publicly is especially pronounced in a world where private belief is fine, so long as you keep it private. For many of us, the fear of offending someone or ruining a relationship often keeps us silent. Yet the words of Charles Spurgeon convict me: "If Jesus is precious to you, you will not be able to keep your good news to yourself. . . . It cannot be that there is a high appreciation of Jesus and a totally silent tongue about him."[6]

Atheist celebrity Penn Jillette sounds a similar note from a different perspective:

> I don't respect people who don't proselytize. . . . If you believe that there's a heaven and a hell, and people could be going to hell or not getting eternal life, and you think that it's not really worth telling them this because it would make it socially awkward . . . how much do you have to hate somebody to *not* proselytize? How much do you have to hate somebody to believe everlasting life is possible and not tell them that?[7]

Sharing one's faith can be uncomfortable, but it is doable. To get past the fear and awkwardness, we must first grasp why our faith is worth sharing in the first place. It is not just good news; it's the best news! We must be confident in the gospel (Phil. 1:4–6), trusting that we may do the speaking, but God does the saving. We don't have to be eloquent or perfect (1 Cor. 2:3–5); the Holy Spirit empowers us (Mark 13:11; John 14:25–26).

In our everyday lives we should pray for open doors to speak about our faith. I recently went to a coffee shop on a Saturday morning to read, and as I walked in, I prayed specifically that the Holy Spirit would use the book I was reading (*Knowing Jesus through the Old Testament* by Christopher Wright) as a bridge to share my faith with a stranger. Sure enough, about thirty minutes into my reading time, a woman sitting near me said, "That's an interesting book you're reading!" This led to a great discussion about Jesus and Christianity (she was a self-described "seeker" when it came to religion), ending with my invitation for her to visit my church. Was it super comfortable to talk to a stranger in a coffee shop about the gospel? No. But it was beautiful to be used by the Holy Spirit in whatever he was doing in this woman's heart.

Sometimes all it takes is a simple prayer before walking into a coffee shop. God *wants* to use us in his mission, but we have to be willing, attentive, and open to his leading. We have to be like Philip in his encounter with the Ethiopian eunuch (Acts 8:26–40): ready for random, uncomfortable encounters and able to speak biblical truth when the opportunity arises. Even Calvinists should pray for this! As Keller puts it, "The next person you pray for and/or share the gospel with may be one of God's elect, and *you* may be part of the way God has ordained to bring them to faith."[8]

Mission Is Costly

One of the most uncomfortable aspects and yet crucial signs of healthy mission is the presence of hard goodbyes. God is a sending God. He sent Jesus to earth. Jesus sent out his disciples. Disciples send out other disciples. Churches are always sending, multiplying, and planting. This keeps the gospel moving and expanding, but it comes with a cost.

Healthy churches are about "gathering and scattering," holding in tension the values of tight-knit community and the sending necessity of frequent goodbyes. A few years ago, Kira and I led a particularly family-like life group of about fifteen single young adults. These men and women were as tight as any group of young adults could be; they would linger at our house for hours after the Bible study ended, and numerous times throughout the week they would get together to hang out with each other. It would have been easy to just keep this special group together over many years, developing a deep, lasting community with them. It would have been sweet. But mission called us to say goodbye. We wanted to launch a new life group out of ours, so we sent two of our best guys, Andrew and Micah, to be the leaders of that new group. Two others, Brent and Mitch, joined a team being sent to plant a church in Thailand. It was hard to say goodbye, and to recognize that the rare chemistry of that group was, in the end, rather fleeting. But it was right. Sometimes the ties that bind must be loosened for the sake of the gospel.

The relational cost of mission also includes potentially forsaking allegiance to family when it conflicts with Christ's call. Jesus said things about family (Matt. 8:21–22; Luke 9:59–60; 11:27–28) that were countercultural, particularly given his Middle Eastern Jewish context, where family identity was everything. The only explanation for Jesus's scandalous commands to repudiate family bonds, says N. T. Wright, "is that he envisaged loyalty to himself and his kingdom-movement as creating an alternative family."[9] This can be a hard thing for Christians who come from families who may not share fervor for mission. The cost for someone called to overseas mission is only amplified, for example, when they have family and friends who think it's a crazy, irresponsible, and cruel move. Confounding family in pursuit of mission is part of its uncomfortable cost.

There are other costs. There is the cost of resources, for example. Missionary life, church planting, and serving the poor . . . these things don't pay well. Missionaries often trade high-paying jobs and suburban comforts for unpredictable reliance on others for financial support, housing, or even food. It's a vulnerable thing to depend on the mercy and generosity of others, but it is the expectation Jesus sets up (e.g., Matt. 10:9–11). This also means that those who stay have a responsibility to be generous and give financially, even if it means sacrificing some comforts.

Being on mission can also be hazardous to one's health. Two of my cousins struggled with health issues while living as missionaries in China, where the extreme pollution and bad air, food, and water can cause all sorts of bodily irregularities. Missionaries and aid workers in politically volatile places in the world routinely put their lives at risk. Think of Samaritan's Purse doctor Kent Brantley, who in 2014 barely survived Ebola after treating patients in Liberia; or Tom Little, a missionary optometrist who was killed by the Taliban in Afghanistan while bringing eye care to a remote part of the country; or the scores of Syrian Christians who have been burned alive, beheaded, and crucified by ISIS in recent years. Being a follower of Christ on mission in a hostile world is not for the faint of heart.

Mission Is Often Mundane

As exotic and dangerous as much of it may be, we must not conceive of mission as only that which takes us far from home or into harm's way. Too often, would-be missionaries are energized by the possibility of going across the world to minister to unreached people groups but are not energized by the prospect of going across town to engage in cross-cultural mission with local, unreached immigrant or minority communities. Young, restless church leaders are writing books and attending conferences about urban ministry in London, New York, or Buenos Aires. But who is getting excited about planting churches in Midwestern suburbia, rural Appalachia, or the tiny towns that dot the farmland in "flyover country"? Arguably, these forgotten, unsexy frontiers of mission are some of the places where gospel-centered, Spirit-empowered church planting is most needed.[10]

Why is it easier for us to go to the other side of the world than it is to go across the street to talk to our neighbors about Jesus? It's uncomfortable to share our faith with people in our immediate context because we have to continue to do life with them and it may get awkward if we bring up Jesus. Plus, it is sometimes easier to care for the soul of the foreigner we don't know than the proven heathen that we do. But if we don't approach our day-to-day lives, neighborhoods, workplaces, and relationships through the lens of mission, we're doing it wrong. Mission isn't just something made possible by a passport or a seminary degree. It's a paradigm that should inform everything we do.

"Everything a Christian and a Christian church is, says and does should be missional in its conscious participation in the mission of God in God's world," says Christopher Wright.[11] This includes the sometimes-uncomfortable task of widening our notion of mission to include our secular work, whether we are lawyers or teachers or stockbrokers or baristas. It includes the dignifying of mundane "mission" at home: being good mothers, fathers, children, siblings, roommates, neighbors. It also includes the uncomfortable call to commit to a local church and focus most of our missional energy therein. This means asking of the church, "What is the need here, and how can I help fill it?" rather than "Here is how I'd like to serve; can you accommodate this?"

This may not be sexy or self-actualizing. But to commit to and simply *serve* in a church—without anyone noticing or without selfies and exotic stories to show for it—is a beautiful thing. There is something countercultural and revolutionary in a church simply being a church, a community of actively serving members practicing resurrection in their neighborhood or city. There is a powerful witness in this, even if it doesn't involve explosive growth, the conversion of celebrities, or some sort of ten-year plan for seven new church plants.

It's not that we should lower our expectations or squelch the ambitious visionaries in our midst. It's just that sometimes the most effective mission is the patient, quiet, unheralded: the sixty-year-old pastor who led his congregation in rural North Dakota for forty years, helping innumerable broken people find healing and hope in Jesus without ever having started a blog or attended a Catalyst conference; the thirty-nine-year-old insurance sales-man who only has sixty-two Twitter followers but has led three children and two coworkers to the Lord; the stay-at-home mom who volunteers at a battered women's shelter three days a week and organizes meals for the needy families in the congregation; the fourteen-year-old girl who resists the cattiness of junior high cliques by seeking out and getting to know the unpopular kids.

There are many "ordinary" ways to be ambassadors of the extraordinary gospel, but none more important than building up the body of Christ by committing to a local church, however bor-ing it may seem. As Kevin DeYoung says,

> In the grand scheme of things, most of us are going to be more of an Ampliatus (Rom. 16:8) or Phlegon (v. 14) than an apostle Paul. And maybe that's why so many Christians are getting tired of the church. We haven't learned how to be part of the crowd. We haven't learned to be ordinary. Our jobs are often mundane. Our devotional times often seem like a waste. Church services are often forgettable. That's life. . . . Life is usually pretty ordinary, just like following Jesus most days. Daily discipleship is not a new revolution each morning or an agent of global transformation every evening; it's a long obedience in the same direction.[12]

The church is imperfect, messy, maddening, and at times mun-dane. But she is the body of Christ, the organism God has chosen to physically manifest the Son to the world by the power of the Holy Spirit.

It may not sound exciting. It may seem too predictable and institutional and bourgeois. It's certainly not going to be comfort-able. But showing up at church week after week, and giving oneself to the building up of the body, is a revolutionary act of mission.

PART 2

UNCOMFORTABLE CHURCH

8

Uncomfortable People

For the body does not consist of one member but of many.

1 CORINTHIANS 12:14

It is impossible to be in Christ and not belong to others. A Christian, by definition, has a connection with and a responsibility to other Christians. You cannot claim Christ and avoid his people.

SAM ALLBERRY

There are some weird people at church. If you've spent any amount of time in a church, you know this. Some of the weird church-people types I have had the hardest time with over the years include:

- The overaggressive huggers who always bypass side-hugging for the full-on hug
- The under-aggressive people who never know whether to hug you or shake your hand
- The Baby Boomer who isn't confident enough to dole out wisdom to Millennials like me
- The know-it-all in life group who "mansplains" everything in a condescending manner

- The external processor who takes up precious social energy by working out meandering thoughts aloud, ad nauseam
- The church lady who manages to ask horribly offensive and personal questions under the guise of kind-hearted concern
- The sweaty-handed people who lay their entire damp palms on your shoulder when they pray for you
- The overly expressive lady who injects bursts of interpretive dance into worship, sometimes with flags like a sort of Pentecostal drill team
- The person who frequently weeps or lies facedown on the church floor during worship, making you feel like an emotionless faux Christian
- The FOMO ("fear of missing out") church members who say they'll be at every event but often flake out at the last minute because something better comes up
- The far-too-happy person whose perpetual smile surely must mask something sinister
- The person who has shaken hands with you twelve times but still can't remember your name
- The guy who thinks every discussion among men must involve meat, beer, cigars, and/or *Every Man's Battle*
- The "I'm not your typical Christian!" churchgoers who go out of their way to cuss and show you their tattoos
- Anyone who talks about the joys of "just doing life together"

The list could go on. And I'm the first to admit that my quirks would probably show up on someone else's list. The point is, we should not expect our church, or any church, to be free of people who annoy us. And that's a good thing.

The reality of God's family is that people have different backgrounds and personalities and opinions. They will clash. It will be messy. It's a huge challenge committing to a family like this, but it is not optional. Adopted sons and daughters of God can't just throw in the towel and retreat to our just-like-me friend groups and homogenous cliques. We must lean into the awkward conglomeration of people who comprise the church.

People Problems

Interpersonal conflict has been part of the church since its earliest days. Think of the rivalry between Peter and John, or the disagreement between Paul and Barnabas in Acts 15:36–41. There's a reason Scripture doesn't hide from these difficulties. The tension of a diverse conglomeration of people coming together in Christ's name will often be combustible, but it's also at the heart of the gospel.

On most Sundays, it's far easier to stay at home than it is to come spend a few hours singing and mingling over doughnuts with people you would never otherwise hang out with. Whether you're an extrovert or introvert, Millennial or octogenerian, Republican or Democrat, you probably find it tough at times to relate to some people in your church. As an introvert, I often dread the "in between" times on Sundays, when I have to muster the social energy to talk to people whose lives and interests are very different than mine. If the pre-church and between-service coffee times at Southlands were full of people who loved Terrence Malick films and cared about Kansas City–area sports, that'd be one thing. As it is, I often struggle to find talking points with the military guys and CrossFit coaches and soccer moms who comprise my community. But I manage, and in the end it is worth it. These are my people. My brothers and sisters. And I love them.

Scott Sauls says membership in a local church means "joining your imperfect self to many other imperfect selves to form an imperfect community that, through Jesus, embarks on a journey toward a better future . . . together."[1] This is the uncomfortable but beautiful struggle of being the church. The church may be faulty, says Spurgeon, "but that is no excuse for your not joining it, if you are the Lord's." Nor should you feel disqualified by your own faults, he adds: "for the Church is not an institution for perfect people, but a sanctuary for sinners saved by Grace, who, though they are saved, are still sinners and need all the help they can derive from the sympathy and guidance of their fellow Believers."[2]

There Is No iChurch

Many Christians today have no problem disengaging from local church life and opting instead for a largely "me and Jesus" faith that only occasionally overlaps with the complex requirements of community.

There have been times in my life when I've gone this route. During graduate school in LA, I attended a large church but never got involved to the point that my absence on a Sunday would be noticed. I was happy to slip in late, sit anonymously in the pew, enjoy the sermon, take communion, and maybe grab a doughnut before I walked briskly to my car.

I can relate to the many who choose this sort of relationship to church. I sympathize with their frustrations with churches and the bothersome types of people who inhabit them. But the Christian life cannot be an individual affair. The church is necessarily plural. To say you "love Jesus but not the church" is to say you prefer a decapitated head. That's creepy and doesn't work biblically (see Eph. 5:23). We are the body of Christ. A head needs a body and a body needs a head. Though it's true there are aspects of salvation and faith that are experienced individually, it's also true that the purpose of the cross "was not just to save isolated individuals, and so perpetuate their loneliness, but to create a new community whose members would belong to [Jesus Christ], love one another and eagerly serve the world."[3]

Part of the challenge for Western Christians is that our environment is radically individualistic. Our loyalties to groups are often rather weak, so we "leave and withdraw, rather than stay and grow up, when the going gets rough in the church or in the home," notes my friend Joe Hellerman in his book *When the Church Was a Family*. But individualism is not the norm of human history: "Most persons who have lived on planet earth have simply assumed that the good of the individual should take a back seat to the good of the group, whether that group is a family, a village, or a religious community."[4]

This approach is countercultural in the "Be who you want to be!" atmosphere of contemporary Western culture, where the autonomy of self reigns supreme. We are more comfortable talking in terms of our "personal relationship" with Jesus than in "we" terms of the corporate health of our faith community. But even though we are called and respond to the gospel on an individual level, we must resist the rampant notion that church is an optional add-on to one's solitary faith journey. Too often we perpetuate an unhealthy disconnect between soteriology and ecclesiology, overlooking the fact that there is a link between being "justified with respect to God the Father upon salvation" and being "familified with respect to our brothers and sisters in Christ."[5]

Individualism conditions us to give preference to our own personal spiritual path, which is not the same as anyone else's and is only slowed, detoured, or muddled when others are enmeshed within it. You see this in the ease with which contemporary Westerners cycle through relationships and ditch friends and family when things get hard.

You also see this in the Millennial aversion to short- and long-term commitments. The dual mind-sets of YOLO ("you only live once") and FOMO ("fear of missing out") lead many young adults to resist being tied down or locked into anything. They want to keep their options open. When it comes to church, they tend to be fickle and prone to switching things up often. To commit to a local church as a for-better-or-worse family, being loyal to it regardless of whether cooler churches or celebrity pastors move in down the street, is truly countercultural. But in my own life, I am seeing that this is the approach that works best, both for the church and for the individuals within it; even if it means we commit to spending a lot of time with people who, let's be honest, we would avoid in any other context.

We Are Stones

One of the ways Western individualism informs how we think about church is that we conceive of "fit" in terms of how a church fits *us*. Does its worship style, architecture, preaching, values, and demographic makeup fit well with our personality and preferences? This approach puts the burden on the church to adapt or perform to our liking if it wants to keep us around. But what if we have it backwards? What if the biblical approach is actually that we should fit *ourselves* into the life and mission of the local church, adapting ourselves to the family and filling gaps where needed, even if that means *we* are the ones who have to change? We shouldn't look for a church that will change to fit us. We should look for one where we will be changed to better represent Christ.

I love the New Testament passages that describe the church in terms of stones. Peter says Christians are "like living stones" who are "being built up as a spiritual house, to be a holy priesthood" (1 Pet. 2:5), with Christ as the cornerstone (2:6–7). Paul says similar things in Ephesians 2:19–22:

> So then you are no longer strangers and aliens, but you are fellow citizens with the saints and members of the household of God, built on the foundation of the apostles and prophets, Christ Jesus himself being the cornerstone, in whom the whole structure, being joined together, grows into a holy temple in the Lord. In him you also are being built together into a dwelling place for God by the Spirit.

The biblical image of the people of God is that we are stones *being built together into a dwelling place*. A dwelling place requires not one big stone but many pieces of stone, interlocked and fortified together. It's not that the stones must lose their individuality or their unique textures or shapes; the image is not one of identical bricks or prefab concrete blocks. It's just that *only together* do individual stones achieve the structural purpose of becoming the household of God. Each of us has unique gifts, but none of us is gifted in everything. Together our unique shapes complement each other and create a more structurally sound "building."

Sadly, our individualistic culture seems more drawn to the "rolling stone gathers no moss" metaphor. Our heroes are the chameleonic artists and celebrities who refuse to be pinned down in style or genre or identity. We love the restless wanderers like Jack Kerouac and rogue subverters of convention like Jackson Pollock. We aren't so compelled by the notion that our "individuality" should be a selfless thing worked out for and within a larger community. Yet that is the biblical ideal. A Christianity that focuses too much on the individual journey and the "How is this growing *me?*" question easily becomes "sourly narcissistic" and "crowds out openness to the Spirit himself," argues Fee.[6] This is one of the reasons why committing to life in community, however uncomfortable it may be, is essential. Individualistic faith shrinks our experience of God and saps the full power of the Spirit in our midst. We thrive most when we live out faith in the presence of the family of God—in all its weirdness and wonderful diversity.

The Messy Beauty of Family Life

So what does it look like in practice to embrace awkward church people as your brothers and sisters, mothers and fathers, sons and daughters in Christ? Hellerman proposes four New Testament "family values" that should guide us: (1) we share our stuff with one another; (2) we share our hearts with one another; (3) we stay, embrace the pain, and grow up with one another; and (4) family is more than "me, the wife, and the kids."[7]

Each of these values carries its own measure of discomfort. Sharing stuff with one another—which includes supporting those in our midst who need financial help or a place to sleep—runs counter to the "my stuff is my stuff" ownership mentality in Western culture. Sharing hearts with one another requires a vulnerability and emotional openness that can also be countercultural, especially when it involves confession of sin.

The "stay and embrace the pain" value is countercultural in a world that encourages people to ditch relationships that are difficult or inconvenient. The family ties of the church should buck the prevailing ethos of loosely bound relationships and strings-attached friendships. Wesley Hill writes about this in his excellent book *Spiritual Friendship*, questioning the sort of friendship that is easily opted in and out of according to personal whims and preferences: "Should we think of [friendship] as preserving its voluntary character and thereby vulnerable at every point to dissolution if one of the friends grows tired of or burdened by the relationship?"[8] Hill's answer is no; brothers and sisters in Christ should be more strongly bonded than that. For Hill, a same-sex-attracted Christian who has committed to celibacy, the importance of family-like community is especially pronounced:

> What I and others like me are yearning for isn't just a weekly night out or a circle of people with whom to go on vacation. We need something more. We need people who know what time our plane lands, who will worry about us when we don't show up at the time we said we would. We need people we can call and tell about that funny thing that happened in the hallway after class. We need the assurance that, come hell or high water, a few people will stay with us, loving us in spite of our faults and caring for us when we're down.[9]

This relates to Hellerman's fourth "family value" about Christian family going beyond "me, the wife, and the kids." The Western church has historically been really bad at this, failing to envision the church family as anything remotely as compelling or important as the nuclear family. The church has perpetuated the American dream of married-with-children life as the ultimate goal.

But for a member of God's family, the white-picket-fenced suburban fortress is *not* the ultimate. As Russell Moore notes, "Every Christian is not called to marriage, but every Christian is part of a family."[10] Christian family life means laying aside our own personal kingdoms and building a "household of God" beyond our nuclear families, with our kinfolk in Christ.

What does this look like? For one, it looks like a more deliberate incorporation of single adults as full-fledged members of the family. Singleness in the church is too often viewed as a struggle to be mourned or a condition to be endured. Scripture says otherwise. In 1 Corinthians 7, Paul argues that singleness is perhaps preferable for believers, except for those who "burn with passion" (7:9). Paul says (7:32–35) to be single is to be focused on the "things of the Lord," whereas marriage requires a focus on "worldly things," like pleasing a spouse. The former allows for undivided attention on God, and the latter is necessarily divided. Married couples in the church ought not to treat singles as second-class citizens in some sort of "waiting room." Singles (following in the footsteps of Paul and Jesus) have much to contribute in the life of the church, not least the important role of helping the church resist idolizing American-dream understandings of flesh-and-blood family. Singles should be included in strategic decision making and as leaders of ministries, as preachers, teachers, life-group leaders, etc. They should be eating meals and hanging out with married couples regularly, not just with fellow singles.

Same-sex attracted singles should be incorporated in all of these ways too. It is especially important that they feel deeply embedded in the family life of the church, able to form intimate friendships with their fellow church members even if it is inevitably complex. This may mean that a clique of young married moms in the church needs to broaden their circle to include the same-sex-attracted woman who doesn't love talking about babies but is in desperate need of female friendship. It may mean that straight men in the church need to forge bonds and share life with same-sex-attracted men in the church who may very well at some point have a crush on them. Talk about uncomfortable! These sorts of relationships will no doubt be awkward and challenging, but they will also be beautiful and countercultural in a world where friendship is framed in path-of-least-resistance terms.

Another way the church should challenge the idolatry of family is through the practice of hospitality. Contemporary Western culture values privacy and personal domains where doors are shut and blinds are closed. But a church family should be characterized by open doors and porous understandings of "home." My friend Vic is a pastor in Toronto and says the Christian call of radical hospitality is a challenge in the Canadian culture. Perhaps it's the "winter hibernation," the "safe approach to relationships," or a fear of subjecting a home's "middle-class treasures to the wear-and-tear of hospitality," says Vic. But whatever the reason, he observes a deep reluctance of many people to open their homes to others.[11]

But hospitality is a crucial part of embracing the uncomfortable people who comprise the family of God. Kira and I decided at the outset of our marriage that our home would have a revolving door and that our table would be frequently full. We make dinner for sixteen in our life group every Wednesday night, and that involves setting up extra tables and chairs, messing up our kitchen, and cleaning up splatters and spills on our furniture. It's worth it. When a young adult in our life group has needed a place to stay, we've offered our guest room. When Christians have visited our church from overseas, we've hosted them. It's been inconvenient at times, but wonderful. Our lives are busy, and we don't keep things as clean as we might like, but we still invite people into our home. Life in the body of Christ need not be about impressing one another or keeping up appearances. It should be about entering one another's spaces often and sharing life together rather than separating into private enclaves as soon as the Sunday morning service lets out.

Sparks of *Sehnsucht*

Sometimes when I go to a Christian conference or visit a church in another city, I meet people with whom the deep familial intimacy of being united in Christ is natural and powerful. It's an instant kinship that offers glimpses of the eternal communion of saints to come. Made all the more poignant by its fleeting, I-might-not-see-you-again-this-side-of-heaven nature, the feeling reminds me of *sehnsucht*, the paradoxical heart-pangs that C. S. Lewis likened to joy: "an unsatisfied desire which is itself more desirable than any other satisfaction."[12]

I've felt this (appropriately) at C. S. Lewis conferences in Oxford and Cambridge, enjoying pub conversation with "mere Christians" from around the world. I've felt it after developing new friendships with believers I met at Q or Together for the Gospel conferences. I've felt it while sitting around a table with pastors in downtown Omaha, or enjoying fish and chips with Christian friends on the ruins of an abbey on England's northeast coast.

Sometimes I come home from these experiences a bit melancholy, wishing that some of these believers from far away could be part of my local, day-to-day church family. They sometimes feel more like kindred spirits than the people in my church family back home. I find myself longing for a family like this, one where people get me and I get them, and the sparks of *sehnsucht* are frequently kindled when we are together.

But the grass is always greener. The truth is, we don't get to choose our perfect local church family. While it is a beautiful thing to connect with Christian brethren for brief moments away from home, our primary church family is our immediate one. To be sure, they are an imperfect bunch, and often maddening. Sometimes the sparks of friction are more common than the "sparks of *sehnsucht*." Sometimes they just feel like aliens to us, and us to them.

But we are aliens together, sovereignly placed together as residents in our community for such a time as this. We are stones being chiseled and smoothed and refined together, and it is painful. But the house the Spirit is building through us is a beautiful thing.

9

Uncomfortable Diversity

For he himself is our peace, who has made us both one and has broken down in his flesh the dividing wall of hostility.

EPHESIANS 2:14

Discipleship is crosscultural. When we meet Jesus around people who are just like us and then continue to follow Jesus with people who are just like us, we stifle our growth in Christ and open ourselves up to a world of division.

CHRISTENA CLEVELAND

It's an embarrassing truth that no one wants to own publicly, but it's true nonetheless: church is more comfortable when you can do it among like-looking, like-minded, and like-everything people. They may not be better, but homogenous churches are easier.

For a few years when I first moved to California, I attended a Presbyterian church in a posh neighborhood in LA. It was a supremely comfortable experience, full of people just like me: white twentysomethings who liked Sofia Coppola films and the music of Sufjan Stevens. When this church announced that it was going to launch a new campus in a gritty and hipster-friendly neighborhood in downtown LA, I signed up to be on the launch team. Urban church planting!

The neighborhood was indeed exciting, and it was fun to enjoy falafel and sushi and speakeasy Scotch bars after Sunday worship services. But the church faced challenges and struggled to grow. We met in a Japanese church's building, and some members of the aging Japanese congregation attended our service. Cultural differences became evident quickly. Vagrants from nearby Skid Row often stumbled into our worship services, smelly and erratic in their behavior. Visitors ran the gamut from hipsters to gay men to Pentecostals and everything in between. The diversity of the people in the services made worship sometimes beautiful in that "foretaste of heaven" sort of way. But often it made community quite challenging.

In this season, I often felt like I couldn't fully relax and experience God through the catharsis of weekly worship alongside people who understood me. On some Sundays I attended a second church service on the other side of town to get my "comfortable church" fix. Eventually I left the church plant because of a job change and move. The next congregation I attended was a lot more homogenous and, naturally, a lot more comfortable.

I understand why we tend toward worship environments that are homogenous or monocultural. Sunday worship is a sacred space, a time in one's week to relax and be *known* and not be burdened by the difficulty of cross-cultural work or the self-consciousness of being a minority. I understand why so many avoid the discomfort of diversity in these sacred times. I understand why, as Martin Luther King Jr. famously noted, 11 a.m. on Sunday morning is the nation's most segregated hour of the week.

I understand it, but I know it's not the biblical ideal.

Diversity Is at the Heart of the Gospel
Believers in the gospel of Jesus Christ cannot be apathetic about diversity, resigning ourselves to voluntary segregation and "doing

church" in our own culturally comfortable ways. Through the cross we are reconciled vertically to God but also horizontally to each other. The latter is not an optional perk. We must recognize (as in Eph. 2:11–22) that the cross destroys the dividing walls of hostility that naturally lead us to avoid or resent one another. The gospel creates a new family, what Platt calls a "multicultural citizenry of an otherworldly kingdom" in which we are empowered by God's grace to "counter selfish pride and ethnic prejudice both in our hearts and our culture."[1]

The messiness but centrality of this occupies much of Paul's writing to the earliest churches. The coming-together-as-new-family of Jews and Gentiles was not natural or practical or precedented. It was crazy. Jews and Gentiles loathed each other. Much of the New Testament is Paul addressing the problems that predictably arose from the somewhat twisted social experiment that was Christianity.

Preaching a gospel of unity-in-diversity was not a recipe for blockbuster church growth in the first century (nor is it now). Yet Paul preached it hard. He said scandalous things (e.g., "There is neither Jew nor Greek, there is neither slave nor free, there is no male and female, for you are all one in Christ Jesus," Gal. 3:28). He knew nothing of homogenous church communities. Rather, he knew that unity-in-diversity was fundamental to God's Trinitarian character, central to the gospel's subversion of hierarchy and ethnocentric pride, and crucial to the church's witness. He knew that communities comprised of natural-born enemies, loving and serving and worshiping one God together, would stop onlookers in their tracks. He knew that the communion of people from every background, every personality, every side of the train tracks, would be the most powerful argument for the gospel.

If the people of God want to live up to their calling as an eschatological community, a present glimpse of the "every tribe and language and people and nation" vision of the future (Rev. 5:9; 7:9), then we have to prioritize diversity. This doesn't mean we downplay our differences or ask every member of our church community to forget their cultures and personalities and backgrounds in favor of some one-size-fits-all set of behavior. Paul's vision of the church is not a melting pot as much as a salad bowl,[2] where the different flavors and textures are all there, complementing one another and working together to create a dynamic, surprising, and beautiful entree.

This includes all different kinds of diversity: ethnic, cultural, gender, age, class, education, personality, political affiliation, and marital status, to name a few. Do we recognize the value of all these forms of diversity in our churches, or are we mostly perpetuating a sameness because it is more comfortable? Are we aware of those in our churches who feel marginalized, unheard, or undervalued? A church leadership team may be full of extroverts, but are they intentionally including and valuing the input of introverts? Who is invisible in our churches? Seekers? Soccer moms? Senior citizens?

Until we recognize the beautiful myriad of diversity that can and should comprise the "we" pronouns of our churches, our "we" will mostly be a narrow and narcissistic extension of "me": church made in my image, with people who look and talk and worship like me. It's more comfortable that way, sure, but it's less biblical.

Six Ways to Prioritize Diversity in Church Life

In theory it sounds great. But how is diversity in the church actually accomplished? First, we must acknowledge that *we* can't accomplish it. Only the Holy Spirit in us can. Only when we fully accept God's grace and mercy to us, and pray for the Spirit to work in our midst, will any of the following be doable. So know the gospel and preach it to yourself often. Then pray. Then consider doing the following:

1) Know your own culture. Recognize it isn't the gold standard.
If churches are going to become more welcoming and inclusive of a diverse array of members, it is vital that church leaders are self-

aware, able to see how their cultural lenses inform the ways they conceive of and practice church. How does American individualism, for example, inform our "my own personal relationship" soteriology and downplay the corporate dimensions of God's plan for his people? How might a white evangelical lens inform the areas of morality and mission that are emphasized? Even in things like music, do we recognize that "Hillsong style" is a particularly young white evangelical style of worship music, and that it is by no means the gold standard? Too often we unknowingly assume that our way of doing church is the way everyone should do it. To break out of this complacency, we should get in the habit of exposing ourselves to other perspectives and church cultures. Maybe a white pastor could attend a Hispanic pastors' conference, or a Pentecostal church member could visit an Anglican church, or a twenty-two-year-old could visit a church full of people in their seventies (or vice versa). Maybe we could reach out to immigrant churches in our communities, serving them but also learning from them. Perhaps we could diversify the blogs and podcasts we take in, and push ourselves to listen more to voices that challenge us. Such things will help us pop our insular bubbles and recognize ways we have conflated cultural identity with Christian identity.

2) Don't whitewash diversity. "Multiethnic ministry" is a buzzword these days and a sincere desire of many evangelical churches. But too often the conversations about multiethnic or multicultural church are led by and on the terms of white evangelicals. Steve Chang, senior pastor of the largely Asian-American Living Hope Community Church in Brea, California, has observed this.

"I think oftentimes multiculturalism is proclaimed as the goal, but often from a white evangelical perspective," he told me. "This is what it is: 'You come to my culture.' It is white culture that they want nonwhites to come and acculturate themselves into, and often they don't realize this is what they're doing."[3]

One way this is manifested is in the tokenism of bringing non-white speakers to white evangelical conferences and giving them the platform to speak (usually only about diversity), but having every other aspect of the conference tailored to the white evangelical culture. Another manifestation is in the well-intentioned but problematic posture of being "color-blind." To downplay racial, ethnic, or cultural differences is to downplay the beauty of the diversity of God's image-bearers and provides an excuse for not leaning in to the discomfort of cross-cultural worship and discipleship.

3) Create a culture of listening, humility, and open conversation. I often get anxious when I talk to my nonwhite friends about issues of race. I fear I will say the wrong thing. I worry that I won't be able to just listen without interjecting or *whitesplaining*. Meanwhile, many people of color, particularly those in predominantly white settings, have anxieties about being ostracized or having their painful experiences invalidated. My friend Phillip, who works with me at Biola and is one of a few black members at Southlands, says that in diverse communities it is important not to establish a culture of guilt, but instead one of humility and forgiveness in Christ. Often cross-cultural conversations go wrong because we respond out of injured pride when we should be responding to injured people, he says. We also need to recognize that every flaw or imperfection is not an indictment of racism or bigotry, he says.

"It's just fallenness, and we're all guilty," he says. "One of the responsibilities of those of us who are not white is to set an atmosphere where our white brothers and sisters can process these things without fear of being cast as a hateful bigot." At the same time, one of the responsibilities of those of us who are white is to set an atmosphere where the unspoken rule of "do this on my terms or not at all" is nullified.[4]

If diversity is going to work, churches need to cultivate an atmosphere of humility and confession and repentance and transparency. Whatever their age, class, gender, or race, people in churches should be free to speak openly to one another about their differences. Everyone should feel heard, surrounded by grace, and united in the cross's call to humility and sacrificial love.

4) Acknowledge privilege and power differentials. I sometimes grow weary of the term *privilege*. Yes, I am a white man who grew up in a stable middle-class family, and I've had many opportunities and advantages. But I've also worked incredibly hard in school and in the workplace. Is that not worth anything? Sometimes I just want to opt out of the whole "privilege" discussion and carry on with my life and work. But that is exactly what privilege is. I can opt out of thinking about systemic advantages and disadvantages if I want to. Minorities can't. I don't have to adjust to any other culture in order to succeed. Minorities do. Because minorities are playing by the majority's rules, they must learn its language and culture in order to survive. Because of all this, it's important for majority-culture Christians to find opportunities in their churches to willingly cede their power and privilege (as Christ did, e.g., Philippians 2). Maybe this means a white church leader gives up his pulpit, occasionally bringing in a nonwhite or global Christian leader to preach. Maybe it means an extroverted alpha-male pastor is quieter in staff meetings and spends more time listening, without comment, to the introverts, women, older men, and minorities on his team. Or maybe it means a team of elders is intentional about seeking out, empowering, and investing in congregants who may not fit the church's typical "leadership mold," but who nevertheless have much to offer.

5) Practice what you preach. It's easy to talk a big talk about diversity. But is there fruit to match our words? I can write three thousand words about the value of diversity in the body of Christ, but what am I doing about it in my own life? Most of us are committed to not being racist, but how are we being *anti-racist*? Most pastors would say they value the contributions of women, but are they actively listening to and empowering women as crucial voices in the church? Most churches would say they desire to foster intergenerational community, but are they willing to respect the wishes of older folks who request the music volume be turned down?

There is a practical intentionality that all of this requires. A tangible discomfort. How can we *practice* diversity in the kingdom of God? Maybe it means our churches make intentional efforts to include diverse worship styles on Sunday mornings. Maybe it means engaging with churches in your city from other cultures, perhaps in a joint worship night or in an ongoing collaborative service project for the community. One practical thing leaders can do is to model cross-cultural relationships in their own lives, cultivating friendships with people who are different from them. Working out the complexities of race in the context of real friendship, after all, is always going to be better than debating it on social media.

I was recently invited to preach at a Korean church in Orange County on a Sunday morning. Kira and I were among the only white people in the church on the day I preached, and I kept thinking, *What if I say something inadvertently offensive?* But it was a beautiful experience, the sort of thing I want and need to be more intentional about: building relationships with and learning from the body of Christ in all of its uncomfortable diversity.

6) Prioritize a diverse leadership staff. One area where church leaders can put their value of diversity into practice is by prioritizing a diverse leadership staff. If white-majority churches want to be more attractive to people of color, having an entirely white leadership team may send the wrong message, for example. As Bryan Loritts points out in *Right Color, Wrong Culture*, the optics of homogenous leadership can be detrimental, especially in a technological era when people can investigate a church online before ever visiting. If they see people on the staff page who all look the same, they may never even physically visit the church.[5]

For Steve Chang, the leadership question is a big one in the "uncomfortable diversity" conversation: "If you're in a dominant white church, to say 'We want Asian Americans to come' is one thing. But would your church welcome Asian Americans and other minorities to such an extent that you would seriously consider them as one of the primary decision makers, to the point that they could make some changes you would be uncomfortable with?" Chang observes that while white Americans have accepted Asian Americans in medicine and education and certain fields, they are still not OK with Asian Americans as their spiritual leaders.

"I've seen communities of aging white congregations in need of a new pastor, and even if there are plenty of qualified Asian-American pastors, they would never think of hiring them," he says. "Some wouldn't even think of having an Asian-American pastor as a guest speaker. They don't look at Asian-American pastors as potential shepherds."

In order to make progress in the area of diversity, homogenous churches (whether white or Korean, mostly twentysomething, or whatever) should seek out diverse voices not only as attendees or occasional contributors, but as leaders.

Chang suggests that when churches have a job or a leadership opening, they should read the demographics of the community they are in and prioritize candidates "who can represent that culture and speak about that culture, and who can change the existing culture to be more effective in reaching that culture."

Too often, though, churches don't hire people like that because while they may be effective in reaching a *new* culture, they won't be the most effective with the *existing* culture. But this is one of the uncomfortable steps churches must take if there is any hope of change. It may mean two steps back, one step forward in the short-term . . . but it will be movement in a more biblical direction.

A Beautiful (but Messy) Mosaic

Diverse churches are beautiful kingdom mosaics that offer glimpses of the *shalom* to come in the new creation, when a perfectly just, harmonious, flourishing city is established. But in the meantime, we live in a world of racism and privilege and bigotry and police brutality and inequality and injustice upon injustice. Diversity is always going to be a challenge in this now-and-not-yet world. Everyone committed to it must accept that diversity is going to mean discomfort.

Progress will be uncomfortable for everyone. For some minorities, the discomfort might be attending a church where they don't feel fully known or understood. Other minorities might feel called into the discomfort of taking a staff position in a church outside their cultural comfort zone, for the sake of helping that church grow toward diversity.

For majority-culture Christians, we have to be willing to engage in uncomfortable situations and relationships and conversations, for the sake of unity in Christ. My friend Phillip compares it with the sacrifice we're called to make in marriage: "Marriage is coming to die. You live in discomfort for the sake of your spouse. We have to live in discomfort for the sake of each other, for the sake of the kingdom. Christ didn't call us to a comfy Christianity. He called us to a cross."

Part of that cruciform call is committing to unity even when cross-cultural conflict, confusion, and discomfort are inevitable.

"If we approached conflict in marriage the way we approach conflict in the church, we would have a 100 percent divorce rate," says Phillip, who is committed to staying at largely white Southlands because he's committed to the unity of the body.

We all need to be committed to that unity, a unity-in-diversity born out of a desire to worship the one God whose image we all bear.

10

Uncomfortable Worship

Oh come, let us sing to the LORD; let us make a joyful noise to the rock of our salvation! Let us come into his presence with thanksgiving; let us make a joyful noise to him with songs of praise!

PSALM 95:1-2

Shared worship is part of what it means when we compare Christianity to a team sport. It is *together* that we are God's people, not as isolated individuals.

N. T. WRIGHT

Worship is where the rubber meets the road in one's willingness to endure the discomfort of local church life.

Worship, after all, is what churches do. They glorify God by teaching, singing, reading, praying, and encouraging one another. But because believers are so conditioned by comfort-idolatry and personal-preference individualism that is the twenty-first-century air they breathe, worship can be a struggle. Each person has a preferred style of music, prayer, communion, liturgy, tithing, and so on, and it can be quite uncomfortable to sit through a worship service that is outside of your preferred mode.

My preferred mode would bear resemblance to the evangelical Anglican worship services I've attended at C. S. Lewis Foundation conferences in Oxford and Cambridge, for example. Beautiful cathedrals. Organ-backed, singable songs that are a mix of ancient sacred music, Victorian hymns, and Stuart Townend songs. A choir. A creed or two. Formal readings of Scripture. Prayers of confession. An expository sermon delivered with passion and poetry. Stained glass. Congregational responses in liturgical cadence. Eucharist (with real wine) that follows a liturgy and is its own substantial section of the service. Passing the peace. A bellowing Bach toccata for organ postlude.

But that's just me. My actual weekly church worship experience at Southlands bears little resemblance to this. And that's OK. Putting aside personal preferences and embracing common, unified, God-centric worship, however uncomfortable it may be, is part of what it means to follow Jesus together. Worship in a "just me and Jesus" sense may be more comfortable, but it is not the biblical ideal. *Corporate* worship is the ideal, and that is always going to be a bit messy.

The Struggle: Sometimes I Want to Run for the Exits

Little fuels the evangelical echo chamber quite like rants about worship. And that makes sense. There are limitless variations to how worship can be done, and one's experience of it is often powerful and personal, for good or ill. Everyone has a culture and a background, and for many people there are things about church from their childhood that they really loved or really hated. Many people have strong opinions about this stuff, and so do I.

Allow me to rant a bit about my own struggles and discomfort with contemporary church worship practices,[1] first about the evangelical church broadly and then about my own dearly beloved local church.

The first thing that irks me about the worship culture in my contemporary evangelical context is how we have both narrowed what worship means in a church setting (basically singing) and also widened it to the point of meaninglessness outside of church (e.g., "I worship by doing Pilates or by watching *Game of Thrones*"). In historical Christianity, worship has included prayer of various kinds, creeds, liturgy, responsive readings, preaching/ teaching, kneeling, silence, confession, prophetic words, instrumental music, the rhythms of the church calendar, and singing. But for most evangelicals today, "worship" is just singing. When and why did we move to such a narrow understanding of worship?

And what about the other extreme, the one represented in Donald Miller's infamous "I Don't Worship God by Singing. I Connect with Him Elsewhere." blog post?[2] Certainly there is a place for a widened understanding of worship as something we do when we glorify God by working within and enjoying his creation.[3] But that kind of worship cannot *replace* the type of worship that happens when the body of Christ gathers for a regular time of Spirit-filled edification. I've heard too many of my Millennial friends say they no longer attend church because they experience God more by hiking in Big Sur or by roasting exceptional coffee beans. But that is the first step to abandoning faith altogether.

I also lament the way architecture and sacred space is ill-considered in much contemporary evangelical worship, with many congregations—even those with the financial means to do better—satisfied to worship in dark, cavernous warehouse spaces or bland rooms with a suburban aesthetic akin to Kohl's.

I lament that the congregational mode in most evangelical worship is essentially "passive audience." Reared in a consumer/ entertainment culture that infiltrates everything, evangelicals today have a far less involved role in church worship than did Christians in ages past. Sometimes the only thing a congregant does in church today is sing, and even then they usually can't hear themselves sing, let alone anyone else, because the volume is so loud.

The music. *Oy*. That's also something I lament. Just as "worship" has been narrowed to basically mean "singing," singing in church has also been narrowed (at least in white evangelicalism) to a very specific, Hillsong-esque form. But why does "worship music" have to feature multiple electric guitars and multiple singers? When and why did this form become the norm? Why are stringed instruments, acoustic styles, gospel choirs, chamber music, and non-Western styles rarely featured in the musical worship of evangelicalism today? Why is it more me- and we-focused than God-focused? Why is 99 percent of it so happy and feel-good in a world full of injustice and sin that should lead us to lament? I'm not a Debbie Downer, and I do think musical worship should generally be a hope-filled and joyous experience, but I often feel missed in a church service that ignores the pain of existence and creation's groaning for restoration.

Which brings me to the worship culture of my current church. Southlands has a charismatic flavor and an energetic, Spirit-filled worship bent. There is a lot of good in this, of course, but some of the church's Spirit-centric worship elements have been tough for me, as I explored in chapter 6. The centrality of prayer of every sort, for example, stretches me. The "pray in groups of three to four people around you" bursts of intimacy-with-strangers, or the larger circles of pre-service prayer, challenges my introverted nature. After the sermon there is often a time where people can come to the front and be prayed for, but my problem with this is that often these important pastoral prayer moments happen while the band is loudly playing the final song. With my low-register, low-volume voice, I often cannot hear myself pray, let alone anyone else in my prayer huddle. It's uncomfortable to have to yell-pray about very personal things into the ear of someone I've just met for the first time.

For me, the discomfort of Southlands worship is encapsulated in the second-Wednesday-of-every-month gathering called 133 (after Psalm 133:1: "Behold, how good and pleasant it is when brothers dwell in unity!"). Life groups from all three campuses meet together for ninety minutes of intense singing and praying, and everyone stands for pretty much the entire duration. The music is loud, energetic, and relentless for a good forty-five minutes or so, and those who would rather sit down after thirty-five minutes can't help but feel guilty for lacking endurance. After singing, the prayer time starts. It sometimes includes open-mic prayers of short bursts of gratitude or adoration, as well as prayer in small groups. Often it includes "kingdom style" prayer, with every person in the room praying aloud simultaneously. At times there is prayer for healing, sharing of prophetic words, or other manner of charismatic expression that would cause many a Presbyterian to run for the exits. Sometimes I want to run for the exits! As an introvert, much of this is the stuff of my nightmares.

But what appears weird to me is likely normal to those who grew up in charismatic churches or the non-Western world. What I see as "wild" worship might seem disappointingly tame to others. For extroverts and charismatically inclined folks, other aspects of worship might be challenging and uncomfortable. Long, doctrinally rich expositional sermons and corporate liturgies of confession might seem dry or dour to a charismatic. Even simple call-and-response elements ("This is the Word of the Lord" / "Thanks be to God" after Scripture reading, or "The peace of Christ be with you" / "And also with you" during the greet-your-neighbor time) feel awkward and uncomfortable to some nonliturgical Christians. On a trip to the UK a few years ago, I took a group from our church to an Anglican Evensong service at St. Paul's in London. While I found the Book of Common Prayer liturgy quite beautiful and worshipful, some from our church found it dead, lifeless, and even disturbing.

We may have different worship-style comfort zones, but we are worshiping the same God. That's why, whether we're a Presbyterian or a Pentecostal, we should not let our worship *preferences* get in the way of our worship *participation*.

The Opportunity: Worship Shapes Us Profoundly

Anyone who has spent time as part of a local church community has likely struggled with some aspects of the worship. But in this discomfort there is also opportunity.

There is the opportunity to exercise humility in the context of community, for one. When it comes to worship styles and preferences, we can go to battle and draw lines in the sand (traditional vs. contemporary, liturgical vs. charismatic), or we can look for ways to listen to and prioritize one other. We may not prefer a certain style of music or way of doing communion, but if others in the community do, this can be an area where we practice sacrificial, deferential love. Knowing that the older congregants in the church love hymns and classical styles, a young worship leader who prefers contemporary songs might opt to feature an old hymn and nonelectric piano periodically. And vice versa. This is something Tyler Braun, a pastor and worship leader in Salem, Oregon, tries to emphasize:

> I want worship to be unifying, and that means valuing various perspectives on congregational worship, trying to incorporate them in ways that fit our team and our church, and teaching the church that part of worship is about serving those around you, not just hearing your favorite song.[4]

Instead of lamenting that something is not our preference and folding our arms in protest over that, perhaps we can humble ourselves and participate anyway. Perhaps we can be open-minded to the diverse ways God's people worship him, and not just tolerate but *participate* in this diversity, learning to love it.

My friend Andrew is a worship leader, and he told me, "There is nothing like stepping into a room of people—four or forty or four hundred—knowing that no matter what songs you sing in what keys or what arrangements, people will sing their hearts out."

What would happen if we put aside our pickiness and just sang our hearts out? This is a definite area of growth for me.

Three years ago when Kira and I started attending Southlands, I complained a lot about the worship. I could hardly bring myself to clap or raise my hands as everyone else seemed so eager to do. It stressed me out. Sometimes I wanted to just retreat to some quiet corner of the sanctuary and pray alone. Yet I committed to the church and committed to having a better attitude about the worship. I began to see how beautiful it is to set aside one's "ideal" for the sake of building unity with others, and soon I began to warm up to the worship style. While it's still a challenge at times, I now find myself looking forward to and being refreshed by the Southlands worship experience, rather than always being exhausted by it. I even raise my hands in worship now, which (as a born-and-raised Baptist) is a big step for me!

The way *uncomfortable worship* has grown me hints at another of the key opportunities of worship in community: spiritual formation. Worship shapes us profoundly. It isn't just an atmospheric adornment to the preaching of theology. It *is* the preaching of theology. The old Latin phrase *Lex orandi, lex credendi*[5] is true. Worship is *derived* from what we believe and is a poetic catechesis for *teaching* us what we believe, shaping our habits and loves and longings in the direction of the kingdom of God. Bodily rhythms of worship have profound shaping potential, and a folded-arms posture forecloses that growth possibility.

Often we approach church worship from a posture of cynicism or apathy. Our heart just isn't in it. And for Millennials, for whom authenticity is a supreme value, nothing is worse than forcing yourself to "go through the motions." But if Christians only ever worshiped when their hearts were "in it" fully, worship would rarely happen. Sometimes "going through the motions" is precisely what we must do. The bodily motions of worship— singing, raising your hands, kneeling, closing your eyes—shape us significantly, even when we don't feel like they are.[6] Committing to showing up and being present and open-hearted in worship is the important thing. It's OK that we don't always have the best attitude about it. By God's grace, the Holy Spirit can work with the weariest, most jaded and passionless souls.

Beyond how it forms us, worship is important because it is a crucial part of mission. Worship and mission are "conjoined twins," suggests N. T. Wright; two components of the "angled mirror" vocation of God's people to "reflect God to the world (mission) and the world back to God (worship)."[7] The practices of Christian worship are countercultural. Think of the church calendar, for example. In orienting worship around seasons like Advent and Lent, giving more attention to Pentecost Sunday than to Father's Day or Mother's Day, for example, a church clearly marks itself out as an *alternative* to the timekeeping rituals of secular life. Worship habits identify Christians in unique ways.

We may assume that the unbelieving world simply sees all of this as weird and cultish and off-putting (which they may). But we must also recognize that there is a supernatural element at work in worship that defies our logical assumptions about what nonbelievers would or would not be attracted to. Christopher Wright puts it this way: "There is an evangelistic power in public worship that declares the praise of God, which cannot merely be equated with personal evangelism, but certainly complements it."[8]

I also think there is magnetism in the joy and energy that comes from the Spirit-filled worship of God's people. As odd as it may be, worship has an undeniable power to lead us to "rejoice with joy that is inexpressible and filled with glory" (1 Pet. 1:8). It fuels the sustaining joy of God's people in a way that is attractive in a world of pain and tribulation. As Martyn Lloyd-Jones states in *Joy Unspeakable*, "That is how Christianity conquered the ancient world. It was this amazing joy of these people. Even when you threw them into prison, or even to death, it did not matter, they went on rejoicing; rejoicing in tribulation."[9]

Don't underestimate the evangelistic power and countercultural joy of worship. It may be weird, but that is precisely where its power lies. People can see that there's something transcendent going on, something that runs counter to the cold rationality and spiritual isolation of contemporary life.

iWorship or God Worship?

As has been highlighted in a variety of ways so far in this book, committing to something *in spite of discomfort* is healthy. Why? Because it challenges the default consumer posture of our culture. The challenge of worship in church community is an especially clear example of this, for the very nature and heart of Christian worship is that it takes us outside the iWorld. Whether or not the style or mode is our preference, God remains worthy of worship. No matter who we are or what we feel. The entire orientation of worship is God-ward, not me-ward.

The vitality of a church's worship depends on members of the body submitting their autonomous freedom and opinionated preferences to the larger community, and ultimately to the Lord. This doesn't mean there is no room for discussion and disagreement and compromise when opinions on songs or eucharistic liturgy clash. But it does mean that in these conflicts we abide by Paul's Ephesians 5 call to a Christlike posture of service and humility ("submitting to one another out of reverence for Christ," v. 21). We glorify God by loving and serving each other in the messiness of worship. This is what Paul tried to communicate to the Corinthian believers, whose worship was often selfish and inconsiderate of others in the community (e.g., eating food sacrificed to idols in 1 Corinthians 8 or Lord's Supper abuses in 1 Corinthians 11).

This sort of humble and submissive posture is the heart and soul of Christian worship because it reflects the deferential character of Christ himself. If worship is ultimately about angled-mirror reflection of God's glory, both upward to him and outward to the world, then the self-giving, others-focused love of our worship is a huge part of this; a love that has no problem bowing the head in deference, opening the hands in release, and relinquishing one's rights for the sake of the King.

11

Uncomfortable Authority

When one rules justly over men, ruling in the fear of God, he dawns on them like the morning light, like the sun shining forth on a cloudless morning, like rain that makes grass to sprout from the earth.

2 SAMUEL 23:3-4

Christian contentment is that sweet, inward, quiet, gracious frame of spirit, which freely submits to and delights in God's wise and fatherly disposal in every condition.

JEREMIAH BURROUGHS

We live in an age that is averse to authority, and understandably so. Authorities we used to trust have time and time again disappointed us. Nations and churches and institutions of all sorts have moved from being trusted organizers of chaos to chaos-amplifying hegemonies prone to dangerous *-isms*. Heroes and icons like Bill Cosby, Lance Armstrong, and Joe Paterno have fallen from grace. The abuse and power-mongering of many pastors and religious institutions have been exposed. The US presidency has gone from being a position of great dignity to being a scandal-ridden reality TV show. And fathers. Where have all the good fathers gone?

It's no wonder we struggle with authority. We should. But leadership failure is only half the problem. Western culture's individualistic consumerism amplifies our resistance to authority. From build-your-own-burrito franchises to customization of media libraries to Amazon's predictive algorithms, everything reinforces a "Have it your way!" idolizing of individual choice and autonomy. It's a world where ceding control or relinquishing sovereign choice for decisions (on everything from blue jeans to gender identity) is unthinkable. A shopper at a clothing store may ask for recommendations from friends in terms of which shirt to buy, or a person ordering food at a restaurant may invite the suggestions of a waiter, but ultimately the decision is the shopper's alone.

This does not work in Christianity. Unwillingness to submit to authority is one big reason people abandon church or create their own custom spirituality. But when one's own personal narrative, experience of God, feelings, and desires provide the only authoritative framework for faith, faith is unsustainable. It becomes a self-locking prison from which there is no exit.

As uncomfortable as it may be in our understandably anti-institutional world, submission to authority outside the self is a necessary and beautiful part of the Christian life.

The Discomfort of Submitting to the Authority of Christ

Christ's authority as Lord, "far above all rule and authority and power and dominion" (Eph. 1:21), is the ultimate and most important authority to which we must submit. But this is easier said than done. It's one thing to call Jesus "Lord." It's another to actually live with our will submitted to his. The challenge boils down to our human propensity to think of ourselves more highly than we ought, believing that we have (or should have) all the wisdom and power that God has.

This propensity goes back to the garden of Eden. Adam and Eve could not accept that they weren't free to be or do whatever they wanted. They could not accept "Hands off!" boundaries around something that they felt was perfectly good.

The first sin and the root of all subsequent sin is the idolatry of self. It is pride, autonomy, control; the inability to accept rules or restrictions on one's freedom. It is knowing the law and disobeying it anyway; knowing God exists and yet not honoring him as Lord (Paul lays it out well in Romans 1:18–32). It is believing we are on par with God and that we needn't defer to his authority.

This temptation is even greater in today's world, where authority is supremely loathed and autonomy supremely celebrated. The lordship of Christ is offensive in a "be who you are" culture of fetishized freedom and "keep your morality out of my bedroom" privacy.

In this context, it is unpopular and uncomfortable to embrace Christ's lordship as a gift. As one blogger recently put it, "In an age of autonomy, it's those who subject their thoughts, behaviors, and passions to an exclusive Sovereign that are the brave few."[1]

But this countercultural embrace of God's authority is counterintuitively freeing. Four hundred years ago, the Puritan Jeremiah Burroughs observed: "Christian contentment is that sweet, inward, quiet, gracious frame of spirit, which freely submits to and delights in God's wise and fatherly disposal in every condition."[2] As I wrote in a recent article, this sort of submission

> is distasteful in our secular age, where the prevailing bourgeois ideal is the right of the sovereign self to determine its identity and destiny, free from any "rules" or requirements. Denying yourself and submitting to King Jesus, then, is true countercultural living. And though it may look like legalism to the world, submitting to his authority is in fact liberty—shocking, unexpected, subversive liberty.[3]

The Discomfort of Submitting to the Authority of Scripture

Part of what it means to submit to the lordship of Christ is being willing to submit to the authority of God's revelation to us in

Scripture. But in what sense is Scripture authoritative? Is it authoritative as a collection of timeless truths and moral teachings? As the definitive historical record of God's work in history? Is it authoritative in that every word of it must be taken literally and every narrative within it taken as indisputable fact? All of these are widely debated questions, which only makes it harder for twenty-first-century people to take Scripture seriously as an ancient authority to which they must submit.

More confusion arises when we start to see the necessary role that interpretation plays in the way Scripture actually functions in the life of the church. When a Catholic or Southern Baptist or Anabaptist talks about the "authority of Scripture," what they implicitly mean is the authority of their particular tradition's interpretation of Scripture. Indeed, the Protestant elevation of *sola Scriptura* has ironically resulted in hundreds if not thousands of subdivisions and denominations and traditions that each acknowledge the authority of Scripture, albeit with different interpretations of what it actually says and means. This becomes problematic when Scripture's authority is invoked as holy justification for the rules and imposed power of human institutions.

But the true authority of Scripture lies not in man but in God the Father, Son, and Holy Spirit. It is the Spirit, after all, who guided its writing and guides us as we read it (1 Cor. 2:12–13; 2 Tim. 3:16; 2 Pet. 1:20–21). Scriptural authority must always be, for us, the authority of God speaking into and guiding our lives rather than us bringing *our* story to Scripture, justifying this or that behavior or ideology or power structure by making hermeneutical leaps. The point of Scripture is to organize the chaos of our reality. It is not for us to organize the alleged chaos of Scripture to fit our preferred reality.

Within the framework of Scripture as God's authoritative blueprint for the flourishing of his people and the larger creation, there can be disagreement and different readings of it. There can (and should) also be a humble acceptance of mystery and paradox.

As Ross Douthat argues in *Bad Religion*, what distinguishes orthodoxy from heresy is "a commitment to mystery and paradox," a comfortability with "the possibility that the truth about God passes all our understanding." Indeed, Christian heresies almost always derive from "a desire to resolve Christianity's contradictions, untie its knotty paradoxes, and produce a cleaner and more coherent faith."[4] It may be more comfortable for us to force Scripture and dogma into "cleaner" boxes, but that almost always leads to trouble. We must let Scripture be Scripture, embracing its tensions and mysteries (e.g., the simultaneous humanity and divinity of Christ, the justice and mercy of God) with patience and humility.

Too often we start not with God's authority but with ours, conveniently turning Scripture into a proof text or a weapon to be wielded in support of *our* blueprints and agendas and preferred conceptions of God. To truly submit to the authority of Scripture is to submit our cultural lenses and worldviews and identity politics to God, prayerfully and humbly using the minds he has given us not to discover what Scripture means *to me* but what it *means*, period; not to see in it what *we* want to see, but what God wants us to see. As Martyn Lloyd-Jones said, "We should not interpret Scripture in the light of our experiences, but we should examine our experiences in the light of the teaching of Scripture."[5]

The Discomfort of Submitting to the Authority of Community

One safeguard against to-each-their-own interpretations of Scripture is community. The authority of community, both in the present tense and across time (tradition), is a guardrail that keeps individuals from veering into heresy. But community is a problematic authority for some, for one big reason: communities are comprised of imperfect people. Tradition too is imperfect; history has many examples of Christian traditions that were dangerously wrong in what they thought was a correct interpretation of Scripture.

And yet submitting to the authority of community is a key part of the Christian life. Whether it is a Christian college requiring students to abide by a set of community standards while enrolled, or a church requiring abstention from certain behaviors (drinking alcohol, perhaps) for would-be deacons, the Christian communities we join provide boundaries and an accountability that is healthy. Where it gets tricky is if we disagree with a policy or theological nuance. If you don't see a biblical case for abstaining from alcohol, and yet you go to a school or a church that forbids alcohol consumption, should you disregard that rule even as a member of that community?

No. It's healthy for us to abide by rules in a community, *even when we disagree with them*. If we voluntarily join a community, we should be ready to submit to the authority of that community's rule, however annoying or uncomfortable it may be.

Submitting to the authority of community also means inviting the community to speak into our lives, our homes, our marriages, our job decisions. In a culture obsessed with privacy and individualism, it is hard to imagine inviting one's community into major life decisions, let alone our marital or parenting struggles. But to *not* do this is to burden ourselves with a no-constraints freedom that often leads to bad decisions and loneliness. Opening our private lives up to the input and support of our church family is a countercultural thing to do in a my-life-is-my-business culture. But it is for our good.

Submitting to the authority of the community means we are humble and teachable rather than arrogant and "I've got this" overconfident. And that goes for the old as well as the young, the seasoned in faith and the green. It means submitting to accountability beyond ourselves. We may grimace a little when we think about accountability partners or when we're asked to break up into small, gender-specific groups in church to talk about things like sex and pornography.

But however inconvenient or uncomfortable it may be, the accountability of the Christian community is a gift. It provides an escape from the prison of autonomy, a community of wisdom and encouragement and burden-carrying love. We should cherish it rather than avoid it. As Dietrich Bonhoeffer said, "It is grace, nothing but grace, that we are allowed to live in community with Christian brethren."[6]

The Discomfort of Submitting to the Authority of Church Leaders

Even if the authority of community in a general sense is palatable, many people today have a hard time accepting the authority of individual church leaders, pastors, or elders. To submit oneself to specific leaders, and to be subject to their correction if necessary, is a challenging prospect for all the reasons already mentioned in this chapter.

I've experienced the challenge of this myself. A few years ago, as part of a leadership development program at Southlands, my wife and I were asked to sit in the front row at church, which is where the elders and their wives sit to help facilitate the worship service. I had a problem with this and made my case to a few of the elders. I argued that sitting in the front row was unnecessary and sent a hierarchical message to the church. One time I sat with Kira in the second row, literally two feet from where the rest of the elders sit. Early in the service one of the elders came over to us and asked us to move up to the front row. We obliged, but I was not happy about it. When I later discussed the incident with the lead elder, I ultimately deferred to his rationale for why leaders sitting in the front row matters. I still may not fully *agree*, but I'm respectfully *submitting* to the elders' wisdom.

Because authority is so unpopular and because the abuse potential is so huge, many pastors and elders shy away from discipline and hard conversations of any kind. But this is unfortunate. Church discipline is biblical (see Matt. 18:15–20; Gal. 6:1–2; Eph. 5:11; 2 Thess. 3:6–15; 1 Tim. 5:19–20; Titus 3:9–11 among others) and has been a crucial part of the entire history of the church.

In the early church, for example, leaders had no qualms about telling new converts that they must abandon behaviors and even professions that compromised their holiness. In a church in Carthage in AD 250, for example, an actor from the local theater converted to Christianity and gave up his profession because the church demanded it. (Christians were not to associate with the theater or the acting profession.) With no income, this believer decided that instead of acting himself, he would just *teach* acting by opening an acting school. This caused a mini-scandal in his church, however, to the point that his pastor, Eucratius, wrote to local bishop Cyprian for advice. Cyprian did not mince words in his response. He forbade this new Christian from even *teaching* acting, as it would be a moral compromise for him and his church community. This no-compromise posture was not without grace, however, as Cyprian did advise Eucratius that the church should support this jobless actor-turned-Christian by providing for his basic needs.

Joe Hellerman tells this story as an example of how normal discipline and authority were in the earliest days of the church, and how much of a contrast it is to Western churches today:

> The early Christians made tremendous demands on their converts—demands that affected the most important areas of their lives. And people came in droves. But we bend over backward in our churches to accommodate the radical individualism of people who come to us to find a "personal" Savior who, we assure them, will meet their every felt need. . . . The Carthaginian church was a church triumphant. Modern evangelicals are a community in crisis. We have much to learn from Eucratius, Cyprian, and their brothers and sisters in the ancient Christian church.[7]

Another lesson we can take from this Cyprian-Eucratius episode is the importance of having overseers and authorities above the local church elders. Pastors need pastors too. They need trusted men who can oversee them and offer them accountability and guidance, whether it be pastors from partner churches, denominational leaders, or others with specified accountability and oversight. At Southlands, for example, the eldership team invites the authority of trusted leaders from other churches both inside and outside our network (Advance). Likewise, our lead elder, Alan, serves as a translocal elder for a few other churches, offering counsel on a range of things and helping with pastoral transitions, elder ordinations, and church-planting decisions. When no congregation is an island and no local church leader purely self-led, the church is better off.

We Need Authority

We need authority in our lives for the same reason we need community. Left to our own devices, we do not flourish. Contrary to the individualistic assumptions of contemporary Western culture, unbridled autonomy is not freeing. It's a prison.

Humans need frameworks, limits, bumpers, models, grids, and guides. God created the family for such a reason. Children need parents who look after them and discipline them and tell them that eating dirt and playing with electrical outlets are things they should not do.

The church family functions in a similar way. Individuals may have decent understandings of themselves, and they may have some nice ideas about "the good life," but such notions (for themselves and for the larger world) are always clearer and better when they are developed in community. We need the perspectives of others. We need others to call us out when our ideas or actions go astray. This is for our flourishing and for theirs.

Our consumerist culture has conditioned us to believe that no one and nothing should ever get between us and what we want. The result is that personal preferences become sacrosanct. But can all preferences coexist without contradiction? What happens if four drivers at a four-way stop all prefer to run through the stop sign? What if one member of a band prefers to play a song in a different key than the other band members? What if one pilot on the LAX tarmac disregards the air traffic control directions because he prefers to do his own thing?

The problem with preferences is that they cannot be absolute. And they are conversation killers. As Miroslav Volf points out, "When possible accounts of a life worth living become mere 'preferences,' the great conversation about that issue grinds to a halt."[8]

We need external arbiters; we need higher-order, bird's-eye view principles to trump our personal preferences. This is true as well for our spiritual formation. We must submit our ideas and preferences about faith and church to God, evaluating them through the grid of Scripture and subjecting them to the evaluation of our larger Christian community. Will this be uncomfortable? Certainly. But in the end, it will help us grow far more than we could if the buck stopped only with us.

12

Uncomfortable Unity

The glory that you have given me I have given to them, that
they may be one even as we are one.

JOHN 17:22

When the church was a family, the church was on fire.

JOSEPH HELLERMAN

The most powerful moments of church unity I have experienced
in my life have almost all happened in the context of the Lord's
Supper: my first all-school communion service during orientation
week at Wheaton College; Eucharist in King's College Chapel in
Cambridge alongside Anglican, Catholic, Orthodox, and evangelical attendees of a C. S. Lewis Foundation conference; a communion service in French at a Reformed church in Paris (complete
with a saliva-drenched common cup); the crackers and juice we
partake together weekly at Southlands.

I don't think it's a coincidence that we feel unified in these
moments. It's called *communion* for a reason, after all. From the
earliest days of the Christian church, the Lord's Supper has enacted the barrier-busting power of the cross to unify diverse people
around the shared nourishment of Christ's body and blood. It's

a unifying power that is mysterious and transcendent, binding us beyond even the bonds of blood relationships. As Wesley Hill writes, "If blood is thicker than water, then Eucharistic blood is thickest of all."[1]

In the church's first centuries, the Lord's Supper was part of a full meal, originally on Saturday nights, modeled in part on the evening banquets that were popular in Greco-Roman culture. But a big difference for these Christian banquets was that poor people were present too. At these meals, the poor and rich rubbed shoulders and shared fellowship, eating the same food and receiving the same bread and wine.[2] It was often messy (see 1 Corinthians 10–11), but it was a picture of what the gospel is and does.

It was a picture of that sober night in the upper room (Matt. 26:20–30; Mark 14:17–26; Luke 22:14–23; John 13–17), when Jesus shared a Passover meal with his closest friends. He broke bread and said, "This is my body, which is given for you" (Luke 22:19). Of the wine he said, "This is my blood of the covenant, which is poured out for many" (Mark 14:24). He told them to love one another, for this would distinguish them as Christ-followers. He washed their feet, modeling the sort of humility such unifying love would require. In this farewell moment of grief and tension, Jesus gave the church a rhythm of embodied unity that would thereafter be our central act of worship: a reminder that our only source of life, love, and unity is the Lamb who was slain, the final sacrifice.

Why Unity Is Important

As uncomfortable as prioritizing unity can be, we must acknowledge that it is nevertheless important. Here are just three reasons why unity is a value we must pursue:

1) It is theologically crucial. Jesus passionately prayed that his followers would be one and "may be brought to complete unity" (John 17:21, 23 NIV). Why? "So that the world may believe that you have sent me" (v. 21). Their unity was rooted in Christ's own unity with the Father, an idea Paul picks up in his own writings about unity and oneness, for example, in Ephesians 4:4–6: "There is one body and one Spirit. . . . one Lord, one faith, one baptism, one God and Father of all, who is over all and through all and in all."

Paul had much to say about the importance of unity as product and proof of the gospel, as we saw in chapter 9, and he underscored it in his regular use of sibling and family language when he was dealing with divisions in churches, whether it be the Jew-Gentile divisions of the Roman church or the status divisions of Corinth (e.g., 1 Cor. 1:10–11; 6:1–8; 2 Cor. 8–9; 13:11). As Joseph Hellerman notes, "If there was one place in the ancient world where a person could expect to encounter a united front, it was in the descent-group family of blood brothers and sisters. For Paul, the church is a family; as such, unity must prevail." One way this is practically embodied is in material solidarity (e.g., Rom. 15:26–27; 1 Cor. 16:1–4; 2 Cor. 8–9). For Paul, this is a tangible expression of the uniting of Jew and Gentile as "siblings in God's eternal family." And "alleviating a brother's poverty is, first and foremost, a family responsibility."[3]

2) It is a powerful witness. A unified church is one of the strongest evidences of the truth of the gospel. This is especially true in a world as fragmented and divisive as ours, where countercultural unity among diverse people stands out. When the rest of the world can't seem to agree on anything or bear to be around people who are different, a church where natural enemies become siblings in Christ is a powerful alternative. Unity is a critical manifestation of a Spirit-empowered church. That's why Paul told the Ephesian Christians to be "eager to maintain the unity of the Spirit in the bond of peace" (Eph. 4:3). It's why he wrote to the Corinthians: "I appeal to you, brothers, by the name of our Lord Jesus Christ, that all of you agree, and that there be no divisions among you, but that you be united in the same mind and the same judgment" (1 Cor. 1:10). Where division might normally reign, unity should instead lead to an uncommon love, where believers listen to and bear with one another. "By this all people will know that you are my disciples," said Jesus, "if you have love for one another" (John 13:35).

3) There is a common enemy. Highs and lows in the history of church unity tend to correspond to the presence or absence of persecution. When things are comfy for the church, it finds reason to squabble and divide. When persecution arises, unity takes on a bit more urgency. As American society secularizes and conservative faith communities become more marginalized, I hope we see a more unified remnant emerge. I've witnessed this a bit in my involvement with religious-freedom challenges facing Biola University and other Christian colleges in California. During the intense fight to ward off a particular state legislative bill, I was part of meetings and strategy sessions with black and Hispanic pastors, Catholic leaders, and others from the diverse cross section of the Christian church. Even though it shouldn't have taken this sort of "foxhole ecumenism" to bring us together, these gatherings were beautiful reminders that we are ultimately on the same team. There is one body, one Spirit, one Lord, one faith, one baptism, one God and Father of all. The challenges we face, the spiritual battles we fight, demand that we embrace the truth that we "are all one in Christ Jesus" (Gal. 3:28).

The Challenge and Limits of Unity

Unity in the church has been a challenging thing since the earliest days of Christianity. The importance of getting Christian belief and behavior right, coupled with the open-to-interpretation nature of much of Scripture, leads to VERY strong feelings and uncompromising convictions on all manner of Christian theology and praxis. Another challenge to unity is geographical and cultural diversity. Unlike other, more regional religions that are buttressed by shared geographical or cultural identity, Christianity has since the beginning been global and transcultural. This means that local cultures and contexts create a multiplicity of Christian identities and permutations. The shape of Christian practice in a Korean megachurch, thus, looks different than a Pentecostal church in Appalachia. Unity amidst such diversity is one of the most brilliant and yet challenging things about Christianity.

This is all exacerbated by the fact that the church is comprised of sinful, difficult people who are prone to pride and division and a preference for "going it alone" in factions and denominations and subcultures that are isolated from one another. It's easier this way, we think. Striving toward unity is a challenge that often seems inefficient and burdensome. As an old saying goes, "If you want to go fast, go alone. If you want to go far, go together." Since Adam and Eve first opted to go it alone outside the rules established for them in Eden, humans have struggled with this temptation. Especially in today's sped-up world, few seem to have the patience for unity. We assume the mission is urgent and there is no time to waste.

There are other unique challenges to unity today. The Internet has made it easier for subcultures and niche faith communities to further entrench themselves. Whether you're a progressive evangelical, a Pentecostal Mennonite, or a "New Monastic" commune with Catholic, Orthodox, and Anabaptist flourishes, the Internet allows you to connect with like-minded comrades and find support for your views. Meanwhile, social media has a tendency to amplify tribalism and encourage constant bickering and intramural battles both within and between these subcultures. Spend any amount of time following Christians on Twitter or in the Facebook comments on a theological article and you will see how divided the church is, how far we are from the "by this all people will know . . . " love that Christ desires for us.

Added to all this is a widespread and warranted skepticism

about unity. When some hear "ecumenical dialogue" or "church unity," they think watered-down theology and Oprah-esque vagaries about love and positivity. Others see warning signs in calls to be a team player. Does holding one's ground on a seemingly small theological point always mean a person is "divisive" and inhibiting unity in the body? The perils of groupthink are real because the rhetoric of unity is powerful and can be easily manipulated. The we-have-a-common-enemy argument has at times been a tactic used by despots and demagogues to consolidate support by playing on fear.

Yet the fact that unity can become problematic is not an argument against pursuing it. The church must wisely embrace the challenge of unity in spite of its potential landmines. But how?

Unity Is Not Uniformity

One reason why unity is challenging is that we think it is an all-or-nothing proposition; that if unity doesn't mean full alignment and togetherness on everything, it doesn't mean anything. This is false. Unity does not require 100 percent agreement on everything. Christians can theologically disagree and still be brethren in Christ, bound together in his love and grace by the power of the Spirit. We can have diametrically opposed political views and yet take the Lord's Supper together. We can stand shoulder to shoulder in mission even if we don't see eye to eye on everything.

But how much theological disagreement can we accept before "unity" is stretched to the point of meaninglessness? Can a Christian who denies the existence of hell be in communion with someone with the opposite view? What sort of unity can exist between LGBT supporters and those who hold traditional views about sexuality and gender? Does agreement with the Apostles' Creed provide a sufficient basis for unity?

We need to first ask: What are we actually talking about *practically* when we talk about unity in the broader Christian church (in the "catholic" sense)? I think we're talking about a unity that, trusting in the Spirit as our "glue" and animating life, can bring us together in action and service and self-defense, even if our beliefs differ on important points. This is the sort of unity that, for example, allows conservative evangelical Protestants to partner with conservative Catholics on legal battles and public policy related to the sanctity of life, religious liberty, and justice, even if they have fundamental theological disagreements on things such as justification.

We also need to talk about essentials and nonessentials. What are the points of doctrine that are crucial for the sort of unity that goes beyond co-belligerence and allows for things like planting churches together or establishing a statement of faith for a Christian school? This is of course a notoriously difficult question, and everyone seems to draw the "core doctrines" boundaries differently.

For example, my church often partners with other churches, both locally and globally, and the elders frequently discuss the question of "essential" doctrinal alignment for the purposes of gospel partnership. We host occasional unity worship nights with a broad array of churches in our city, and the criteria for that grouping of churches is one thing. But when it comes to which churches we partner with in a more formal and sustained way, the criteria is more rigorous. If we are going to pool resources into a common fund for church planting, does it matter that we have slightly different views on the role of women in leadership? These are the sorts of questions we should at least ask as we "make every effort to keep the unity of the Spirit" (Eph. 4:3 NIV).

Unity in the broader body of Christ is important, but as C. S. Lewis articulates in *Mere Christianity*, the actual Christian life is lived out in specific communities. He describes a hall with many doors that open to individual rooms. The hall is "mere Christianity," and all of us should celebrate when a person enters that hall for the first time. But ultimately we must choose a specific room in which we can commit and grow:

The hall is a place to wait in, a place from which to try the various doors, not a place to live in. For that purpose the worst of the rooms (whichever that may be) is, I think preferable. It is true that some people may find they have to wait in the hall for a considerable time, while others feel certain almost at once which door they must knock at. I do not know why there is this difference, but I am sure God keeps no one waiting unless He sees that it is good for him to wait. When you do get into the room you will find that the long wait has done some kind of good which you would not have had otherwise. But you must regard it as waiting, not as camping. You must keep on praying for light: and, of course, even in the hall, you must begin trying to obey the rules which are common to the whole house. And above all you must be asking which door is the true one; not which pleases you best by its paint and paneling.[4]

Unity doesn't mean confusing the hall and the rooms. Distinct rooms that each have different wallpaper and furniture make it a better house. As Douthat puts it: "In an age of institutional weakness and doctrinal drift, American Christianity has much more to gain from a robust Catholicism and a robust Calvinism than it does from even the most fruitful Catholic-Calvinist theological dialogue."[5]

Unity Requires Humility and Love

Commenting on the "hall and rooms" *Mere Christianity* passage, John Piper suggests that Christian unity happens best "when we live well in our communities of conviction, and love well across convictional lines."[6] This is harder than ever to do in our polarized world. It's a love that bears with brothers and sisters in Christ when they frustrate you with their different opinions or preferences. It's a love that doesn't run away from tension and understands that there are many gray areas where grace amid disagreement must prevail. It's a love that empowers a church to balance tensions like Word-Spirit, truth-love, local-global, proclamation-demonstration, and others, even if it would be easier to choose sides on all these spectrums. Embracing (rather than being embarrassed by) the seeming contradictions of Jesus is a key to orthodoxy. Attempting to "extract from the tensions of the gospel narratives a more consistent, streamlined, and noncontradictory Jesus," on the other hand, leads to heresy.[7]

Holding to tension-filled orthodoxy, and attempting unity with people who are different or who disagree with us, requires a huge amount of humility. We cannot come at this with arrogance or a sense of being the gold standard. When Paul urges the Ephesian Christians "to walk in a manner worthy" of their calling, he describes it this way: "with all humility and gentleness, with patience, bearing with one another in love, eager to maintain the unity of the Spirit in the bond of peace" (Eph. 4:1–3). Peter tells Christians to "clothe yourselves, all of you, with humility toward one another" (1 Pet. 5:5).

This sort of humility is perhaps especially critical for leaders, whose power puts them in a dangerous position where they can define unity and boundaries on their terms. Instead, we need models of servant leadership in the mold of Christ (Phil. 2:3–8). Rather than setting the terms according to their comfort and preferences, a Christian leader should relinquish power for the sake of building up unity in the body.

Unity is crucial for the effectiveness of the body. Imagine a body where one leg had a different idea of where to walk than the other, or where the lungs and the kidneys had totally different opinions about how the body should function. The disunity of its many members leads to a broken if not incapacitated body. The brilliance of Paul's body metaphor is that it positions unity in terms of interdependence. Unity exists in the body insofar as the parts—women, men, young, old, introvert, extrovert—recognize that they need one another and humbly work to that end.

The body of Christ is the ideal metaphor for unity because it returns us to the Eucharist, reminding us that whatever unity we might hope for in the *church* body comes only because of *Christ's* body, the "bread of life" that sustains us all (John 6:35) and was broken for us. "Because there is one bread, we who are many are one body, for we all partake of the one bread," wrote Paul to the Corinthians (1 Cor. 10:17). Commenting on the Eucharist in the year 253, Cyprian of Carthage said this:

> By this very sacrament our people [are] shown to be united. Just as many grains, collected and milled and mixed, make one bread, so let us know that in Christ, who is the heavenly bread, there is one body, to which our number has been joined and united.[8]

Though we have many tastes and appetites, aversions and allergies, the food we all need more than anything is this "heavenly bread." Though it would be easier and more comfortable to segregate according to those who prefer rye over sourdough, pita over puff pastry, gluten or (in the case of my wife) gluten-free, in the end we are called again and again back to the bread of life. In this we find unity: not where our taste buds lead us, but where our hunger is truly satisfied.

13

Uncomfortable Commitment

And let us consider how to stir up one another to love and good works, not neglecting to meet together, as is the habit of some, but encouraging one another, and all the more as you see the Day drawing near.

HEBREWS 10:24-25

How easy is it for an American Christian to approach finding the right church the way we approach buying cereal at the supermarket? We're looking for all the right ingredients and rejecting churches because they don't have our style of worship, our style of preaching, or our types of people. We're purchasing a product rather than committing to the body of Christ.

SOONG-CHAN RAH

Back in the introduction to this book I wrote: "A healthy relationship with the local church is like a healthy marriage: it only works when grounded in selfless commitment and a nonconsumerist covenant."

Now in the penultimate chapter I want to contemplate this idea further, as I think the challenge and beauty of uncomfortable church is very similar to the challenge and beauty of marriage.

That is, the challenge of both finding the right spouse and then sticking with that spouse for better or worse.

First, the challenge of finding the right spouse.

You may have wondered at various points in this book, "I get that we shouldn't be too picky with church, but we still *do* have to pick a church. If not because it is a good fit for me and my needs and preferences, what criteria should I use to pick a church?"

Good question.

There is no such thing as the perfect church, but there are certainly good ones and bad ones. There is no simple formula for finding the right church in your community, just as there is no simple formula for finding the right spouse.

Before Kira and I started dating, I had ideas about what I was looking for in a wife. I wanted a wife who loved reading Marilynne Robinson novels and watching Terrence Malick films as much as I did. I wanted a wife who was excited by the prospect of leaving sunny California to live in cold, rainy Oxford or Edinburgh for a while. I wanted a wife who enjoyed spending Saturdays reading and napping and discussing divine foreknowledge.

But Kira wasn't any of those things. She wasn't who I had pictured being with, but the more I got to know her the more I came to see she was the best wife for me. And I was the best husband for her. We weren't necessarily the most *compatible*, but we were a great *combination*. Our differences complemented and stretched the other.

Compatibility matters when it comes to finding a spouse, as it does when finding a church. But it isn't everything. Commitment matters more than compatibility. Dating is a good process of discernment, but if it's only about discerning "the perfect fit for me," it will be an endless and ultimately disappointing search. At some point we just have to commit, recognizing that we aren't perfectly compatible but we are perfectly covered by the grace of God and perfectly empowered by the Holy Spirit to make it work. "We don't marry soul mates," says pastor Alan. "We marry suitable strangers." The same goes for "marrying" a church. But how do we determine a "suitable" stranger?

In the introduction I proposed this: "What if we committed to the nearest nonheretical, Bible-believing church where we could grow and serve—and where Jesus is the hero—however uncomfortable it may be?"

Nonheretical. Bible-believing. Opportunity for growing and serving. Jesus as hero. Those criteria are a good start. C. S. Lewis adds a bit more in his "hall and rooms" passage:

> In plain language, the question should never be: "Do I like that kind of service?" but "Are these doctrines true: Is holiness here? Does my conscience move me towards this? Is my reluctance to knock at this door due to my pride, or my mere taste, or my personal dislike of this particular door-keeper?"[1]

Is holiness there? Does my conscience move me toward this place? Good criteria. Lewis also suggests paying attention to what repels us and why. Taste and personal dislike are not good reasons to stay away.

Often the way a church challenges us or makes us uncomfortable is precisely the reason why it is good for us. That has been the argument of this book. Rather than excuses to leave or break up, perhaps we should lean in to the aspects of the relationship that make us squirm. Perhaps we should lean in to the challenge and discomfort of committing to an imperfect and sometimes infuriating church.

Of course there are limits to this. If "leaning in" to the discomfort of a relationship with a church only breeds bitterness and conflict and abuse, then of course "breaking up" is advisable and justifiable. No one should stay in an abusive relationship, and sometimes the line between a highly uncomfortable environment and an unhealthy or unsafe environment can be blurry. We need to be willing to leave if things are constantly toxic and not getting better, but we shouldn't confuse discomfort and dysfunction. Too often we leave a church the minute things get challenging, missing out on the edification that good discomfort can bring.

Good discomfort is a refining process, both in relationships with people and in our relationship with a church.

For Better or for Worse

Picking the right spouse is just the warm-up for the real challenge of marriage. The hard part is sticking with the spouse and being faithful to covenantal vows. Even when our spouses change (and we do too). Even when it is arduous and inconvenient. Even when we get bored and more attractive options present themselves.

The same goes for sticking with a church.

The ease with which Christians "break up" with a church these days reflects Western society's relational woes. Church commitment in America is fragile for the same reason marriage rates are declining: people are more skeptical than ever of long-term commitments and less willing to risk a union with a partner who is not the perfect fit. In 2012, 1 in 5 American adults ages twenty-five and older had never been married, while in 1960 only 1 in 10 adults had never been married. The median age for first marriage in 2012 was twenty-seven for women and twenty-nine for men, while in 1960 it was twenty for women and twenty-three for men. Why this increased reluctance to get married? Pew reports that among those who aren't married but desire to be married, 3 in 10 say the main reason they aren't married is that they "have not found someone who has what they are looking for in a spouse."[2]

Desire for perfect compatibility is a problem. And that makes sense for a generation that has grown up in a consumerist society where there are limitless options of brands and apps and genres and communities that can be tailored and curated in a perfect-for-me sort of way. And that's the same mentality informing our approach to church.

Furthermore, the low-commitment mentality toward church

parallels our cultural acceptance of no-fault divorce. We separate and go our own ways as soon as it becomes inconvenient. And as we discussed in chapter 5, the church's permissive attitude toward divorce has greatly undermined its witness. If the message a church sends is "No-fault divorce is fine!" then how can it complain when a longtime church member goes through a mid-faith crisis and starts "dating" the hip, more attractive church down the street?

What would happen if we had higher expectations of commitment, both in marriage and in church? Christena Cleveland puts it this way:

> Theoretically, married people can't quit a marriage. In the same way, theoretically, Christians can't quit the body of Christ. . . . Our submission to God, irrevocable commitment to each other and interdependence should hold us together when we want to distance ourselves from Christians who fail to live up to our gold standards or who complicate our lives.[3]

What if we took seriously our "for better or worse, till death do us part" vows in marriage and also applied them to church? What if we loved our spouses and loved the church like Christ does?

The church as a bride is not just a random, pleasant metaphor in Scripture. It is of profound theological importance. It is how God relates to his people. "The church is the beloved bride of Jesus," writes Sam Allberry. "Church is not his hobby; it is his marriage—and it's ours too."[4]

We see it in the Old Testament when God made a covenant with Israel and was faithful to the union, even when Israel was unfaithful. Much of the story of Israel is the story of a chronically unfaithful wife, a runaway bride who, as one author recently put it, "has an affair on the honeymoon."[5] And yet God is faithful. He keeps pursuing this runaway bride. He ultimately sends his Son to take the punishment for the bride's infidelity so that her shame and impurity can turn to virginal beauty once again and the marriage can be restored.

In Ephesians 5:22–33, Paul famously compares husbands and wives to Christ and the church. He says things like "the husband is the head of the wife even as Christ is the head of the church, his body" (v. 23) and "Husbands, love your wives, as Christ loved the church and gave himself up for her, that he might sanctify her, having cleansed her by the washing of water with the word, so that he might present the church to himself in splendor, without spot or wrinkle or any such thing, that she might be holy and without blemish" (vv. 25–27). This passage foreshadows Revelation's visions of a perfected bride: at the marriage supper of the Lamb, for example (Rev. 19:7–9), or as the New Jerusalem described as "a bride adorned for her husband" (21:2), "the wife of the Lamb" whose radiance is like "a most rare jewel, like a jasper, clear as crystal" (21:9–11).

This cosmic romance between the Bridegroom (Christ) and his bride (the church) is hinted at and reflected in the way marriage between men and women should be, argues Paul. A husband should love, nourish, and cherish his wife as he would his own flesh, because that is how Christ treats the church, his body. The one-flesh union of a man to his wife, Paul argues, is just like Christ and the church, the head and the body, in a "profound mystery."

Can We Have Jesus without the Church?

Ephesians 5 is often looked to as an instructive passage for marriage, and it is. But I think it is also an instructive passage about the church, especially in an age where many evangelicals have a take-it-or-leave-it ecclesiology somewhere between "I love Jesus but not the church" and "I'll go to church but only as long as it meets my needs."

When Paul says, "Christ is the head of the church, his body," it is a statement of union, of one-flesh connectedness. A head is necessarily connected to a body. The head directs the body and has authority over the body but also *needs* a fully functioning body for effective movement in the world. In a profoundly mysterious way, Christ has humbly attached himself to an imperfect body (those who believe in him) and loved this body, filling it with his sanctifying Spirit so that it will be perfected for that future moment of "without spot or wrinkle" glory. In the meantime, the church is still imperfect.

Sadly, the still-imperfect nature of the church proves too challenging for some. They prefer to be "spiritual but not religious." They embrace Jesus but ditch the church, oblivious to the fact that in so doing, they are creepily embracing a decapitated head. Or those who do recognize the importance of the biblical idea of church simply redefine "church" on their terms. These are the people who love saying, "You don't *go* to church. You *are* the church." This is Donald Miller, who says he connects with God more outside of church and says, "The church is all around us, not to be confined by a specific tribe."[6] This is Rob Bell, who now believes church is simply doing life in a beach community with one's "little tribe of friends" ("We're churching all the time").[7]

But how much can we really grow when we define church on our terms, within the framework of our preferences and proclivities and with a "tribe" of people who "connect with God" most by surfing and enjoying craft beer together? As R. C. Sproul says, "It is both foolish and wicked to suppose that we will make much progress in sanctification if we isolate ourselves from the visible church."[8]

Or listen to Spurgeon, who is (God bless him) characteristically blunt about the matter:

> I believe that every Christian ought to be joined to some visible Church—that is his plain duty according to the Scriptures. God's people are not dogs, otherwise they might go about one by one. They are sheep and, therefore, they should be in flocks.[9]

Can one "have Jesus but not the church?" Not really. If we are in union with Christ, the head, then we are necessarily also connected to his body, the church. "Christ utterly identifies with his people," says Allberry. "Neglecting the church is neglecting Jesus."[10]

Our real choice is this: Do we want to be *plugged into* the life-blood and energy of the body, or do we want to cut ourselves off from this body, lying inert somewhere as a severed finger or amputated leg? The upside of being a severed finger is, you don't have to bother with cooperating with the other fingers, annoying as they are. The downside is, you can't really do anything, and you have no biological connection to the neuron signals coming from the head.

Post-Consumer Christianity

The sort of "spiritual but not religious," churchless iFaith that I've just described is not only unbiblical; it's also bourgeois. Though it may have at one point been countercultural, today a detachment from organized religion for a self-defined spiritual "path" is in no way subversive. It's quite normal and safe and boring and main-stream. As Ross Douthat points out, the "God Within" consumer spirituality of America today does not serve as a corrective or critique to leisure-class comfort, but rather as an affirmation of it:

> For all their claims to ancient wisdom, there's nothing re-motely countercultural about the Tolles and Winfreys and Chopras. They're telling an affluent, appetitive society exactly what it wants to hear: that all of its deepest desires are really God's desires, and that He wouldn't dream of judging.[11]

Ultimately this sort of narcissistic, on-my-terms spirituality isolates us and undermines our ability to be refined by others in a manner we could never accomplish ourselves. This sort of faith, unshackled from the burdens of community, "promises content-ment, but in many cases it seems to deliver a sort of isolation that's at once comfortable and terrible—leaving us alone with the universe, alone with the God Within."[12]

This is a sad form of faith. A faith of isolation has nothing prophetic to say or revolutionary to offer to a world of isolation. Loneliness is everywhere today, amplified by a social-media dynamic that blurs the lines between consumerism and human connection. Relationships (whether marriages, friendships, or members within a local church community) are weakly bound and subject to the fickle disposability of what Pope Francis calls a "culture of the ephemeral," in which people move rapidly from one affective relationship to another.

> They believe, along the lines of social networks, that love can be connected or disconnected at the whim of the consumer, and the relationship quickly "blocked." I think too of the fears associated with permanent commitment, the obsession with free time, and those relationships that weigh costs and benefits for the sake of remedying loneliness, providing protection, or offering some service. We treat affective relationships the way we treat material objects and the environment: everything is disposable; everyone uses and throws away, takes and breaks, exploits and squeezes to the last drop. Then, goodbye.[13]

Against this backdrop, the church can be relevant and countercultural not by reinforcing unencumbered individualism, but rather by challenging people to connect and commit to the body of Christ.

Millennials are commitment averse. They (we) don't like to be pinned down or locked into anything, whether a career or dwelling place or church. We are the FOMO ("fear of missing out") generation, preferring to keep our options open rather than committing to something or someone and foreclosing other possibilities. We are the generation that has rendered RSVP-based party planning a futile endeavor. We are the generation that is opting to own homes at a far lower rate than previous generations did. The vast majority of us (91 percent) expect to stay in a job less than three years.[14] We are less likely to be affiliated with a religion or a political party than previous generations were.

A youth pastor recently told me a story that illustrates how the FOMO mentality manifests itself in church. The youth group was going on a weekend camping retreat and students had signed up a couple weeks in advance. A few nights before they left, the youth pastor got a call from a parent. The parent simply said, "My daughter found out about another event happening this weekend at a church her friends go to. She wants to go to that one instead." The youth pastor challenged the parent. "But she is a member of *our* youth group and she committed to coming with us on our trip." The parent continued to justify her daughter's last-minute switch, citing her wishes to hang out with a group that was a better relational fit.

Comfort over covenant. But for followers of Jesus, it should be the other way around.

Covenant over Comfort

If the church is going to thrive in the twenty-first century, she needs to be willing to demand more of her members. She needs to assert the importance of covenants over comfort, even if that is a message that will turn off some. She needs to speak prophetically against the perversions of cultural and consumer Christianity, seeker-unfriendly as that will be. She needs to call Christians away from an individualistic, "just me and Jesus" faith, challenging them to embrace the costliness of the cross and the challenge of life in a covenantal community.

Covenants are never easy and rarely comfortable. Every marriage testifies to this, as does the roller-coaster history of "prone to wander" Israel. Yet covenants do something that is far more constructive than anything comfort can do. Covenants challenge us to bear with and sacrifice for the sake of others, for the glory of God. Covenants provide necessary checks on the freedoms we might think are liberating but are ultimately constrictive: to follow my heart wherever it leads; to engage or disengage from others whenever it's convenient; to have no moral limits beyond what I establish for myself. Covenants free us from the prison of unlimited freedom.

I attended a Christian college (Wheaton) and have worked at one (Biola) for the last nine years. These schools have "community covenants" that students and staff agree to, conduct policies that preserve the distinctly Christian character of the campus community. Though often derided and unappreciated by students in the midst of them, these policies are undeniably crucial and counter-cultural. In an age where applying uniform behavioral norms to a diverse group of people is anathema and "do no harm to others" is the only consensus moral imperative, asking twenty-one-year-olds on a college campus to not drink alcohol and not have sex is straight-up absurd. But it is an absurdity that provides an all-too-rare check on the idol of autonomy.

Speaking to a room full of Christian college presidents, *New York Times* columnist David Brooks praised the character-shaping value of covenants:

> For most of us, our inner nature is formed by that kind of covenant in which the good of the relationship takes place and precedence over the good of the individual. For all of us, religious or secular, life doesn't come from how well you keep your options open but how well you close them off and realize a higher freedom. Hannah Arendt wrote, "Without being bound to the fulfillment of our promises, we would never be able to keep our identities. We would be condemned to wander helplessly and without direction in the darkness of each person's lonely heart, caught in its contradictions and equivocalities."[15]

Covenants free us from the arbitrary confusion of our fickle hearts. Covenants bind us, in beautiful ways, to the hearts of others and the heart of Christ. And in that binding we discover more clearly the sort of being we were created to be. Covenants teach us that keeping promises to others is more important than being true to yourself.

Covenants are not comfortable, but they are comforting. In our age of isolation and ephemerality, to commit to a Christian community is to remove from ourselves the heavy burden of aimless purpose and amorphous identity. And so I end this chapter by calling the body of Christ to renewed commitment.

For pastors and church leaders: Will you commit to confidence in the gospel rather than condescension to the consumers you hope to reach? Will you commit to leading with, rather than apologizing for, the offense of the cross? Will you commit to raising the bar for your flock rather than lowering it, calling them to Jesus-like holiness rather than affirming their "authenticity"? Will you commit to joyfully building an uncomfortable church?

And for churchgoing Christians: Will you commit to joining and sticking with a church, not because it is a *good fit* for you but because it is *fitting you* to become more like Jesus? Will you commit to looking at church not in terms of what you can get but what you can give, considering how your presence with the body might encourage others and stir them to love and good works? Will you embrace the awkwardness and inconvenience and uncool costliness of the uncomfortable church?

14

Countercultural Comfort

Let us rejoice and exult and give him the glory, for the marriage of the Lamb has come, and his Bride has made herself ready.

REVELATION 19:7

The glory of the gospel is that when the church is absolutely different from the world, she invariably attracts it.

MARTYN LLOYD-JONES

Seeker-friendly Christianity tried to revive the church by infusing it with the logic of the marketplace. Hipster Christianity tried to revive the church by obsessing over newness and relevance. Both of these approaches were efforts to address Christianity's PR problem, attempting to convince an increasingly secular population that Christianity isn't as weird, stodgy, traditionalistic, legalistic, homophobic, judgmental, anti-intellectual, regressive, and conservative as they thought it was. An admirable goal, to be sure.

Yet as typically happens, the pendulum with these approaches swung too far in the other direction, to the point that Christianity became more about apologizing for itself and affirming the culture than about extolling Christ and transforming the culture.

Rather than pointing confidently to the way of Christ, the church has narcissistically critiqued itself and praised the culture, all while Christ is relegated to a supporting-actor role. In our echo chamber we've busily churned out books and blog posts about all the things we're bad at and all the ways we can learn from *Breaking Bad*, Buddhism, David Foster Wallace, and [insert a *Zeitgeisty* pop-culture item here]. But apparently we're too bored (or ashamed) to bother with what we can learn from the Bible (ugh, so clichéd!).

Instead of celebrating the fact that Christianity has contributed good things to the world for two thousand years, the increasingly unpopular church feels the need to talk only about the bad things she has done. Rather than drawing from her rich heritage of time-tested tradition, today's church chooses to adopt last week's fashion so as to be *relevant* again.

We've become bored with our story, or just ignorant of it, and so naturally others have too. We're a bride who forgets why she fell in love in the first place. We're a bride who often takes off her wedding ring in public. We've lost eyes to see the loveliness of the covenant we are in because we're too preoccupied with how skeptical onlookers see us. We assume the only way hipsters and seekers and anyone else might like us is if we offer a "safe place" Christianity, one with endless caveats, asterisks, apologies, and trigger warnings (and fair-trade coffee).

Yet seeker-friendly and hipster Christianity failed to invigorate contemporary Christianity because they've been too embarrassed to lead with the admittedly uncomfortable truth that a Christianity with no teeth, no offensiveness, no cost, and no discomfort is not really Christianity at all. It attracts the masses to something vaguely moralistic and therapeutic, but mostly just affirms their "eat whatever fruit you want" freedom and status-quo comfort.

On the contrary, uncomfortable church is what grows and stretches and builds the body of Christ to be effective in the world.

It may be seeker-unfriendly, but it will be friendlier to seekers in the long run because it will actually transform them.

———

Seeker and hipster Christianity are forms of comfortable Christianity. Comfortable Christianity is not going to change your life. It's not going to make a dent in the world.

The church that *will* change your life is the one that challenges you to grow rather than affirms you as you are. The church that will change the world is the one that provides a refreshing alternative to, rather than an uncritical affirmation of, the way things are. Rod Dreher says the best witness Christians can offer a post-Christian culture "is simply to be the church, as fiercely and creatively a minority as we can manage." To survive what he calls "the new Dark Age," Dreher says today's churches must stop "being normal" and must commit more deeply to the faith, "in ways that seem odd to contemporary eyes."[1]

Faithful Christians should embrace rather than be embarrassed by their abnormal status and strange practices; not for the sake of being weird, but for the sake of the world. As I wrote a few years ago, "Christianity's true relevance lies not in the gospel's comfortable trendiness but in its uncomfortable transcendence, as a truth with the power to rebuff, renew, and restore wayward humanity at every epoch in history."[2]

A couple years ago I received an email from a reader who described himself as a "lapsed, lazy, backsliding, and confused" Christian. He wrote:

> I don't want church to be a mirror image of my life, in all its uncertainty and weakness. I want church to be church, to be challenged, to disagree (not be cozily affirmed), to be my refuge and my rock. I may be someone who cusses from time to time myself, who gets drunk, who has done lots of things

I shouldn't have done (and still do), but that doesn't mean I want to be seeing those things where I (very occasionally) worship. The point of church and faith is that they are sanctuaries from ourselves, they are places where we can lay it all down and know that God hears us, that he forgives us, and that we are only saved by his grace.

This is the revolution of Christianity. It redefines comfort as something that is actually the opposite of how a consumer-oriented society defines it. Christianity announces that true, transcendent, lasting comfort is available to anyone, but not on the terms we might prefer, and not as a reward for our tireless efforts to earn it.

I think the Beatitudes (Matt. 5:3–11) capture it well. In these eight famous statements from the Sermon on the Mount, Jesus outlines the countercultural "comfort" that characterizes his kingdom:

In a "God Within" world where self-sufficiency reigns and depravity is downplayed, Jesus says we must recognize our spiritual neediness in order to enter the kingdom: "*Blessed are the poor in spirit, for theirs is the kingdom of heaven*" (v. 3).

In a world that avoids unpleasantness and prefers celebrating human potential to lamenting human evil (both in systems and in ourselves), Jesus says true comfort comes by mourning sin: "*Blessed are those who mourn, for they shall be comforted*" (v. 4).

In a survival-of-the-fittest world that promises mansions and Maseratis to the ambitious winners who look out for themselves and push their way to the top, Jesus promises a greater inheritance to those who eschew egocentricity: "*Blessed are the meek, for they shall inherit the earth*" (v. 5).

In a consumerist world that promises satisfaction on the other side of desire (for sex, for entertainment, for travel, for things), Jesus promises satisfaction for those who desire obedience to God's will: "*Blessed are those who hunger and thirst for righteousness, for they shall be satisfied*" (v. 6).

In a bitter world where we are constantly offended, judged,

and wronged both by our friends and our enemies, Jesus says we can be freed to forgive because we have already been forgiven by him: "*Blessed are the merciful, for they shall receive mercy*" (v. 7).

In a world that says you can only see your true self by breaking free of the restrictive, patriarchal apparatus of a religious "purity" regime, Jesus says you will see God by being purified by his blood and seeking him with an undivided heart: "*Blessed are the pure in heart, for they shall see God*" (v. 8).

In a dog-eat-dog world of war and terrorism and scandal and grievance, where ideologies and identities are constantly doing battle, Jesus says those who enter the fray for the sake of cultivating peace will be in his family: "*Blessed are the peacemakers, for they shall be called sons of God*" (v. 9).

And in a world that privileges self-preservation and autonomy above transcendent truth and costly obedience, Jesus says the kingdom belongs to those who suffer for their godly living and Christlike convictions: "*Blessed are those who are persecuted for righteousness' sake, for theirs is the kingdom of heaven*" (v. 10).

Perhaps in our familiarity with these words we've become numb to their audacity. Perhaps they've become too ingrained in the ether of polite society (and thus neutered) to inspire us anymore.

But if the church is to thrive in the twenty-first century, she must recover the jarring and profound paradoxes of what Christ calls her to embody: a kingdom where last is first, giving is receiving, dying is living, losing is finding, least is greatest, poor is rich, weakness is strength, serving is ruling.[3]

It's a kingdom where worldly comforts are nothing compared to the power of the Comforter in us; where all manner of uncomfortable things are endured for righteousness' sake.

It's a kingdom of salt and light, which is to say a kingdom of *difference*. Salt is worthless if it loses its flavoring and preservative function. Light is valuable only insofar as it is a contrast to the darkness around it.

The church needs to see all of this not as an embarrassment or an albatross, but as a privilege and a joy. We need to be in *awe* of it, wowed by it, compelled by its immensity. Every time the plate of wafers and juice passes down our pew; every time we grab the sweaty hand of our neighbor to pray; every time we sing the praise chorus refrain for the SIXTY-SEVENTH TIME as if in the Hillsong equivalent of *Groundhog Day* . . . we must see that it is all miraculous. The Creator of the universe is in our midst, present in the mess of it all.

Regardless of its routine, the reality of the church is revolutionary. However unpopular we are, our purpose is profound. As salt and light, we are the hope of the world.

We are, mysteriously, part of a cosmic plan God has eternally known. And we have an eternal inheritance. The discomfort and disdain we endure in this life as a peculiar people will be a blip in the timeline of our infinite history. We will at last be the perfect church we presently long for; the unblemished bride at an unimaginable wedding feast.

The dream will be real.

Acknowledgments

This book was inspired by my experiences in local churches, and my gratitude begins with Southlands Church. I want to thank the many brothers and sisters there who read chapters, listened to my ideas, and supported the book's creation. The support, friendship, and pastoral leadership of Alan Frow has been especially valuable to me. I want to also thank Andrew Scherer, Dave Covarrubias, Albert Rios, Jason Newell, Brian Bowman, Jon Boone, Luke Phillips, Jeremy Hamann, Phillip Wallace, Ryan MacDonald, the Southlands eldership team, and all the life group members who have sat in our living room over the years and heard me talk about the ideas in this book.

There are many other church families I'd like to thank: Cornerstone in Newcastle, City Gates in Toronto, Citylight Benson in Nebraska, Living Hope in Brea, Cross of Christ in Costa Mesa, Lenexa Baptist in Kansas, and all the church communities I have called home in my life. Each of you has shown me something new and beautiful about the bride of Christ.

Speaking of bride, I am grateful as ever to Kira, my partner in life and ministry and every discomfort that comes. She was the first reader of every word in this book.

Others who have played key roles in the creation of this book: Erik Wolgemuth, Dave DeWit and the Crossway team, Russell Moore (for writing an amazing foreword!), my friends and colleagues at Biola University, everyone I interviewed over email or in person, the extended McCracken and Williams families, and the excellent baristas at Hopper & Burr, where I spent many hours writing. I'm grateful to all of you!

Notes

Introduction

1. See "Vision and Values," Redeemer Presbyterian Church, accessed November 8, 2015, http://www.redeemer.com/learn/about_us/vision_and _values.
2. As in Abraham Kuyper, the Dutch Calvinist thinker who believed God worked within and was sovereign over every aspect of human existence.
3. Charles Spurgeon, "The Best Donation" (No. 2234), delivered on April 5, 1891 at the Metropolitan Tabernacle in London, England, http://www .spurgeongems.org/vols37-39/chs2234.pdf.
4. I realize that this is easier said than done, and that the process of finding a church like this still involves important discernment and consideration of factors. For more on what to consider in a healthy "church search," see chapter 13.

Chapter 1: Embrace the Discomfort

1. Ed Stetzer, "Survey Fail—Christianity Isn't Dying: Ed Stetzer," *USA Today*, May 14, 2015.
2. Christian Smith and Melina Lundquist Denton, *Soul Searching: The Religious and Spiritual Lives of American Teenagers* (Oxford University Press, 2005).
3. Terry Eagleton, *Culture and the Death of God* (New Haven, CT: Yale University Press, 2014), 147.
4. Russell Moore, "Is Christianity Dying?" *Moore to the Point* (blog), May 12, 2015, http://www.russellmoore.com/2015/05/12/is-christianity -dying/.
5. Ibid.
6. C. S. Lewis, "Answers to Questions on Christianity," in *God in the Dock* (Grand Rapids, MI: Eerdmans, 1970), 58.
7. "Do Hard Things: A Teenage Rebellion against Low Expectations," The Rebelution website, accessed January 20, 2017, http://therebelution.com /books/do-hard-things/.

8. Alan Kreider, *The Patient Ferment of the Early Church: The Improbable Rise of Christianity in the Roman Empire* (Grand Rapids, MI: Baker Academic, 2016), 149.

Chapter 2: The Uncomfortable Cross

1. George Bennard, "The Old Rugged Cross" (1913).
2. John R. W. Stott, *The Cross of Christ*, 20th Anniversary Edition (Downers Grove, IL: InterVarsity Press, 2006), 221.
3. Friedrich Nietzsche, *The Antichrist*, in *The Portable Nietzsche*, ed. and trans. Walter Kaufmann (New York: Penguin, 1977), 572, 634.
4. Stott, *The Cross of Christ*, 45.
5. Nabeel Qureshi says that the "litmus test" between Christianity and Islam comes down to "the issue of whether Jesus died on the cross" in his book *Seeking Allah, Finding Jesus* (Grand Rapids, MI: Zondervan, 2014), 146.
6. Dietrich Bonhoeffer, *The Cost of Discipleship* (New York: Simon & Schuster, 1959), 89.
7. Stott, *The Cross of Christ*, 159.
8. Bonhoeffer, *The Cost of Discipleship*, 44–45.
9. For more on this topic, see Brett McCracken, *Hipster Christianity: When Church and Cool Collide* (Grand Rapids, MI: Baker, 2010). Much of what follows is taken from the "Cool vs. Christianity" chart in *Hipster Christianity*, 199.
10. Russell Moore, *Onward: Engaging the Culture without Losing the Gospel* (Nashville: B&H, 2015), 7.
11. Stott, *The Cross of Christ*, 338.
12. N. T. Wright, *Jesus and the Victory of God* (Minneapolis: Fortress, 1996), 405.
13. Adam S. McHugh, *The Listening Life: Embracing Attentiveness in a World of Distraction* (Downers Grove, IL: InterVarsity Press, 2015), 162.
14. Scot McKnight, *A Fellowship of Differents: Showing the World God's Design for Life Together* (Grand Rapids, MI: Zondervan, 2015), 228.
15. Christian Wiman, *My Bright Abyss: Meditation of a Modern Believer* (New York: Farrar, Straus & Giroux, 2013), 155.
16. C. S. Lewis, *Mere Christianity* (San Francisco: HarperSanFrancisco, 2001), 226–27.

Chapter 3: Uncomfortable Holiness

1. Those written thoughts eventually became my book *Hipster Christianity: When Church and Cool Collide* (Grand Rapids, MI: Baker, 2010).
2. I explored the healthy balance between the two extremes in Brett McCracken, *Gray Matters: Navigating the Space between Legalism and Liberty* (Grand Rapids, MI: Baker, 2013).
3. Jonathan Lunde, *Following Jesus, the Servant King: A Biblical Theology of Covenantal Discipleship* (Grand Rapids, MI: Zondervan, 2010), 50.
4. Ibid., 172–73.

5. Rod Dreher, *The Benedict Option: A Strategy for Christians in a Post-Christian Nation* (New York: Sentinel, 2017), 19.

6. Alan Kreider, *The Patient Ferment of the Early Church: The Improbable Rise of Christianity in the Roman Empire* (Grand Rapids, MI: Baker Academic, 2016), 13. Kreider illustrates this focus on behavior and habitus by quoting early church leaders like Cyprian: "We know virtues by their practice rather than through boasting of them; we do not speak great things but we live them" (p. 13). Or Lactantius on a non-coercive missional strategy that is focused on embodying truth: "We use no guile ourselves, though they complain we do; instead, we teach, we show, we demonstrate" (p. 34).

7. Russell Moore, *Onward: Engaging the Culture without Losing the Gospel* (Nashville: B&H, 2015), 8.

8. Much of this section and the next are taken directly or adapted from my article "Has 'Authenticity' Trumped Holiness?," The Gospel Coalition (blog), January 26, 2014, https://www.thegospelcoalition.org/article/has-authenticity-trumped-holiness-2.

9. Josh Riebock, "Fighting for Authenticity," *Relevant*, Oct. 1, 2007, http://www.relevantmagazine.com/god/deeper-walk/features/1292-fighting-for-authenticity.

10. Nick Bogardus, email interview with author, December 13, 2015. Used with permission.

11. Megan Hill, "The Very Worst Trend Ever," *Christianity Today*, July 8, 2013, http://www.christianitytoday.com/women/2013/july/very-worst-trend.html.

12. Scott Sauls, *Jesus Outside the Lines: A Way Forward for Those Who Are Tired of Taking Sides* (Carol Stream, IL: Tyndale, 2015), 105.

13. C. S. Lewis, *Mere Christianity* (San Francisco: HarperSanFrancisco, 2001), 225.

14. John R. W. Stott, *The Cross of Christ*, 20th Anniversary Edition (Downers Grove, IL: InterVarsity Press, 2006), 275.

15. Nick Bogardus, email interview with author, December 13, 2015. Used with permission.

16. Stott, *The Cross of Christ*, 277–78.

17. Lunde, *Following Jesus, the Servant King*, 274.

Chapter 4: Uncomfortable Truths

1. Russell Moore, *Onward: Engaging the Culture without Losing the Gospel* (Nashville: B&H, 2015), 5.

2. Owen Edwards, "How Thomas Jefferson Created His Own Bible," *Smithsonian* magazine, January 2012, http://www.smithsonianmag.com/arts-culture/how-thomas-jefferson-created-his-own-bible-5659505/.

3. Rachel Held Evans, *Evolving in Monkey Town: How a Girl Who Knew All the Answers Learned to Ask the Questions* (Grand Rapids, MI: Zondervan, 2010), 92–93.

4. Timothy Keller, "3 Objections to the Doctrine of Election," The Gospel Coalition (blog), September 21, 2015, http://www.thegospelcoalition.org /article/3-objections-to-the-doctrine-of-election.

5. Rob Bell, "Rob Bell—*LOVE WINS: A Book about Heaven, Hell, and the Fate of Every Person Who Ever Lived*," YouTube video, March 2, 2011, https://youtu.be/ivwfqBNICf4.

6. Richard Dawkins, *The God Delusion* (Boston: Houghton Mifflin, 2006), 31.

7. Christopher Hitchens, *God Is Not Great: How Religion Poisons Everything* (Toronto: McClelland & Stewart, 2008), 102.

8. Paul Copan, *Is God a Moral Monster? Making Sense of the Old Testament God* (Grand Rapids, MI: Baker, 2011), 188.

9. William Lane Craig, "Slaughter of the Canaanites," *Reasonable Faith* (blog), August 5, 2007, http://www.reasonablefaith.org/slaughter-of-the -canaanites.

10. This is discussed in chapter 3 of Paul Copan and Matthew Flannagan, *Did God Really Command Genocide? Coming to Terms with the Justice of God* (Grand Rapids, MI: Baker, 2014), 37–47.

11. C. S. Lewis, *The Problem of Pain* (New York: Macmillan, 1962), 118.

12. Tim Keller, *The Meaning of Marriage: Facing the Complexities of Commitment with the Wisdom of God* (New York: Dutton, 2011), 221.

13. In 2007, for example, the Barna Group found that 91 percent of non-Christian and 80 percent of churchgoing young people saw Christianity as anti-gay. See David Kinnaman and Gabe Lyons, *UnChristian: What a New Generation Really Thinks about Christianity* (Grand Rapids, MI: Baker, 2007).

14. Tyler Braun, email interview with author, January 29, 2016. Used with permission.

15. Keller, *The Meaning of Marriage*, 221.

16. Scot McKnight, *A Fellowship of Differents: Showing the World God's Design for Life Together* (Grand Rapids, MI: Zondervan, 2015), 127.

17. N. T. Wright, *After You Believe: Why Christian Character Matters* (New York: HarperOne, 2010), 250.

18. McKnight, *A Fellowship of Differents*, 128.

19. Richard B. Hays, *The Moral Vision of the New Testament: A Contemporary Introduction to New Testmament Ethics* (New York: HarperOne, 1996), 392.

20. David Platt, *Counter Culture: Following Christ in an Anti-Christian Age* (Carol Stream, IL: Tyndale, 2015), 166.

21. Hays, *The Moral Vision of the New Testament*, 382.

22. Ibid., 389, 395.

23. Ibid., 388.

24. John Piper, "For Single Men and Women (and the Rest of Us)," *Desiring God*, July 1, 1991, http://www.desiringgod.org/articles/for-single-men -and-women-and-the-rest-of-us.

25. Scott Sauls, *Jesus Outside the Lines* (Carol Stream, IL: Tyndale, 2015), 145.

Chapter 5: Uncomfortable Love

1. Scot McKnight, *A Fellowship of Differents: Showing the World God's Design for Life Together* (Grand Rapids, MI: Zondervan, 2015), 58.
2. Richard B. Hays, *The Moral Vision of the New Testament: A Contemporary Introduction to New Testament Ethics* (New York: HarperOne, 1996), 348.
3. Jim Hinch, "Evangelicals Are Losing the Battle for the Bible. And They're Just Fine with That." *Los Angeles Review of Books*, February 15, 2016, https://lareviewofbooks.org/essay/evangelicals-are-losing-the-battle-for -the-bible-and-theyre-just-fine-with-that/.
4. C. S. Lewis, *The Four Loves* (London: Collins, 1960), 111.
5. David Wells, *God in the Whirlwind: How the Holy-Love of God Reorients Our World* (Wheaton, IL: Crossway, 2014), 95.
6. David Platt, *Counter Culture: Following Christ in an Anti-Christian Age* (Carol Stream, IL: Tyndale, 2015), 138.
7. All quotes in this paragraph are James K. A. Smith, "Marriage for the Common Good," *Comment*, July 17, 2014, https://www.cardus.ca /comment/article/4247/marriage-for-the-common-good/.
8. Josef Pieper, *Faith, Hope, Love* (San Francisco: Ignatius Press, 1997), 187.
9. David Wells, *God in the Whirlwind*, 85.
10. Ibid., 86–87.
11. See Barry Corey, *Love Kindness: Discover the Power of a Forgotten Christian Virtue* (Carol Stream, IL: Tyndale, 2016).
12. Joshua Ryan Butler, *The Skeletons in God's Closet: The Mercy of Hell, the Surprise of Judgment, the Hope of Holy War* (Nashville: Thomas Nelson, 2014), 189.
13. John R. W. Stott, *The Cross of Christ*, 20th Anniversary Edition (Downers Grove, IL: InterVarsity Press, 2006), 127.
14. Wells, *God in the Whirlwind*, 81.
15. Quoted in David Von Drehle, "How Do You Forgive a Murder?" *Time*, November 12, 2015, http://time.com/time-magazine-charleston-shooting -cover-story/.
16. C. S. Lewis, *Mere Christianity* (San Francisco: HarperSanFrancisco, 2001), 86.
17. *The Works of the Emperor Julian*, vol. 3, trans. W. Wright, in Loeb Classical Library (London: W. Heinemann, 1923), 17, 69.
18. Peter Scholtes, "They'll Know We Are Christians," © 1966, F.E.L. Publications, assigned to the Lorenz Corp., 1991.

Chapter 6: Uncomfortable Comforter

1. Sam Storms, *The Beginner's Guide to Spiritual Gifts* (Minneapolis: Bethany House, 2012), 10–11.

2. Gordon Fee, *Paul, the Spirit, and the People of God* (Grand Rapids, MI: Baker Academic, 1996), 82.

3. Ibid., 105.

4. Ibid., 10.

5. Ibid., 177.

6. Cessationists often point to 1 Corinthians 13:9–10 ("but when the perfect comes, the partial will pass away") as justification that the "partial" (charismatic gifts) ceased when the "perfect" (the Bible) came. But continuationists dispute this interpretation of the word "perfect."

7. Storms responds to this by arguing that the mediation of the miraculous through human instrumentality is not about the person's power as much as it is "about God, at his time and according to his purpose, imparting a gift or enablement to a particular person on a particular occasion to accomplish a particular purpose" (Storms, *Beginner's Guide*, 105).

8. Ibid., 11.

9. Francis A. Schaeffer, "The Lord's Work in the Lord's Way," in *No Little People* (Wheaton, IL: Crossway, 2003), 74.

10. Daniel Wallace admits to bibliolatry, "The Text Became My Idol," in *Who's Afraid of the Holy Spirit? An Investigation into the Ministry of the Spirit of God Today*, eds. Daniel Wallace and M. James Sawyer (Dallas: Biblical Studies Press, 2005), 8.

11. Timothy J. Ralston, "The Spirit's Role in Corporate Worship," in *Who's Afraid of the Holy Spirit?*, 130.

12. Terry Virgo, *The Spirit-Filled Church: Finding Your Place in God's Purpose* (Oxford: Monarch Books, 2011), 43, 44.

13. Daniel B. Wallace, "Introduction: Who's Afraid of the Holy Spirit? The Uneasy Conscience of a Non-Charismatic Evangelical," in *Who's Afraid of the Holy Spirit?*, 2, 11.

14. M. James Sawyer, "The Father, the Son, and the Holy Scripture?" in *Who's Afraid of the Holy Spirit?*, 275.

15. Wayne Grudem, *Who's Afraid of the Holy Spirit?*, 284–85.

16. Piper quotes in this section are from Tony Reinke's article, "Piper Addresses Strange Fire and Charismatic Chaos," Desiring God, November 16, 2013, http://www.desiringgod.org/articles/piper-addresses-strange-fire-and-charismatic-chaos.

17. Virgo, *The Spirit-Filled Church*, 120.

18. Storms does say that for some "believers only" meetings, small-group home gatherings, or other events where no unbelievers will be turned off (1 Cor. 14:22–23), uninterrupted tongues can be appropriate. "If there were a gathering of Christians exclusively for the purpose of worship and prayer, a gathering in which the circumstances that evoked Paul's prohibitions of uninterpreted tongues did not apply, would the prohibitions stand? I'm inclined to think not" (*The Beginner's Guide*, 173–74).

19. Ibid., 152.

20. Virgo, *The Spirit-Filled Church*, 75.
21. Martyn Lloyd-Jones, *Westminster Record* 43, no. 9, quoted in Virgo, *The Spirit-Filled Church*, 72.

Chapter 7: Uncomfortable Mission

1. Christopher J. H. Wright, *The Mission of God's People: A Biblical Theology of the Church's Mission* (Grand Rapids, MI: Zondervan, 2010), 30.
2. Ibid., 78.
3. Ibid., 94.
4. Pope Francis, *Encyclical on Climate Change and Inequality: On Care for Our Common Home* (Brooklyn, NY: Melville House, 2015), 56–57, 75.
5. David Platt, *Counter Culture: Following Christ in an Anti-Christian Age* (Carol Stream, IL: Tyndale, 2015), 27.
6. C. H. Spurgeon, "A Sermon and a Reminiscence," *Sword and Trowel*, March 1873, http://www.spurgeon.org/s_and_t/srmn1873.php.
7. Penn Jillette, "Not Proselytize," YouTube video, uploaded November 13, 2009, https://www.youtube.com/watch?v=owZc3Xq8obk.
8. Tim Keller, "3 Objections to the Doctrine of Election," The Gospel Coalition, September 21, 2015, https://www.thegospelcoalition.org/article/3-objections-to-the-doctrine-of-election.
9. N. T. Wright, *Jesus and the Victory of God* (Minneapolis: Fortress Press, 1996), 400.
10. On this subject, I recommend Donnie Griggs's book, *Small Town Jesus: Taking the Gospel Mission Seriously in Seemingly Unimportant Places* (Everyday Truth, 2016).
11. Christopher Wright, *The Mission of God's People*, 26.
12. Kevin DeYoung, "Stop the Revolution. Join the Plodders," Ligonier Ministries (blog), September 9, 2016, http://www.ligonier.org/blog/stop-the-revolution-join-the-plodders/.

Chapter 8: Uncomfortable People

1. Scott Sauls, *Jesus Outside the Lines: A Way Forward for Those Who Are Tired of Taking Sides* (Carol Stream, IL: Tyndale, 2015), 47.
2. Charles H. Spurgeon, "The Best Donation," (No. 2234), delivered April 5, 1891 at the Metropolitan Tabernacle in London, England, http://www.spurgeongems.org/vols37-39/chs2234.pdf.
3. John R. W. Stott, *The Cross of Christ*, 20th Anniversary Edition (Downers Grove, IL: InterVarsity Press, 2006), 249.
4. Joseph H. Hellerman, *When the Church Was a Family: Recapturing Jesus' Vision for Authentic Christian Community* (Nashville: B&H Academic, 2009), 4.
5. Ibid., 132.
6. Gordon D. Fee, *Paul, the Spirit, and the People of God* (Grand Rapids, MI: Baker Academic, 1996), 127.
7. Hellerman, *When the Church Was a Family*, 145.

8. Wesley Hill, *Spiritual Friendship: Finding Love in the Church as a Celibate Gay Christian* (Grand Rapids, MI: Brazos Press, 2015), xv.

9. Ibid., 41–42.

10. Russell Moore, *Onward: Engaging the Culture without Losing the Gospel* (Nashville: B&H, 2015), 180.

11. Quotes from personal email interview with author, March 14, 2016. Used with permission.

12. C. S. Lewis, *Surprised by Joy: The Shape of My Early Life* (New York: Harcourt, 1955), 17.

Chapter 9: Uncomfortable Diversity

1. David Platt, *Counter Culture: Following Christ in an Anti-Christian Age* (Carol Stream, IL: Tyndale, 2015), 209.

2. Scot McKnight uses the metaphor of a salad bowl in *A Fellowship of Differents: Showing the World God's Design for Life Together* (Grand Rapids, MI: Zondervan, 2015), 27. One example: "There are different cultures, there are different socioeconomic classes. . . . And they are all together at the table, in the salad bowl, thrashing it out with one another. That thrashing it out is what the church is about—*and that is what the Christian life is all about: learning to love one another, by the power of God's grace, so we can flourish as the people of God in this world.*"

3. Quotes from Chang are from personal interview with author, December 8, 2015. Used with permission.

4. Quoted from a personal interview with author, February 5, 2016. Used with permission.

5. Bryan Loritts, *Right Color, Wrong Culture: The Type of Leader Your Organization Needs to Become Multiethnic* (Chicago: Moody Press, 2014), 38–39.

Chapter 10: Uncomfortable Worship

1. My perspective, like anyone else's, is shaped by my church history. I grew up in a Midwestern Baptist context, where hymns, choirs, and orchestras were the norm but liturgy wasn't. In college at Wheaton, I became aware of Reformed theology and church history and moved in a more Presbyterian direction. After college, I worked for the C. S. Lewis Foundation in Oxford and Cambridge, traveled all around Europe, and fell in love with old forms of worship. I even attended an Episcopal church for a summer! Now I'm at a charismatic Reformed church pastored by a South African. All of this informs my proclivities in worship.

2. See Donald Miller, "I Don't Worship God by Singing. I Connect with Him Elsewhere." *Storyline* (blog), February 3, 2014, http://storylineblog.com/2014/02/03/i-dont-worship-god-by-singing-i-connect-with-him-elsewhere/.

3. I argued this in my book *Gray Matters: Navigating the Space between Legalism and Liberty* (Grand Rapids, MI: Baker, 2013).

4. Tyler Braun, email with author, January 29, 2016. Used with permission.

5. "*Lex orandi, lex credendi*" is loosely translated "The law of praying [establishes] the law of believing," essentially meaning, "As we worship, so we believe."

6. James K. A. Smith's books—*Desiring the Kingdom, Imagining the Kingdom,* and *You Are What You Love*—are very helpful explorations of these concepts.

7. N. T. Wright, *After You Believe: Why Christian Character Matters* (New York: HarperOne, 2010), 220, 243.

8. Christopher J. H. Wright, *The Mission of God's People: A Biblical Theology of the Church's Mission* (Grand Rapids, MI: Zondervan, 2010), 250.

9. Martyn Lloyd-Jones, *Joy Unspeakable: Power & Renewal in the Holy Spirit* (Wheaton, IL: Harold Shaw Publishers, 1984), 102.

Chapter 11: Uncomfortable Authority

1. Dustin Messer, "Following Rob Bell: The Edges of Faith and the Center of the Zeitgeist," *Kuyperian Commentary*, November 30, 2015, http://kuyperian.com/following-rob-bell/.

2. Jeremiah Burroughs, *The Rare Jewel of Christian Contentment* (1648; repr., Edinburgh: Banner of Truth, 1964), 19.

3. Brett McCracken, "Lordship Is Not Legalism," The Gospel Coalition website, December 28, 2015, https://www.thegospelcoalition.org/article/lordship-is-not-legalism.

4. Ross Douthat, *Bad Religion: How We Became a Nation of Heretics* (New York: Free Press, 2012), 10, 12.

5. Martyn Lloyd-Jones, *Joy Unspeakable: Power & Renewal in the Holy Spirit* (Wheaton, IL: Harold Shaw Publishers, 1984), 17.

6. Dietrich Bonhoeffer, *Life Together: The Classic Exploration of Christian Community* (New York: Harper Collins, 1954), 20.

7. Joseph H. Hellerman, *When the Church Was a Family: Recapturing Jesus' Vision for Authentic Christian Community* (Nashville: B&H Publishing, 2009), 101.

8. Miroslav Volf, "Life Worth Living: The Christian Faith and the Crisis of the Humanities," Yale Center for Faith and Culture, accessed January 23, 2017, http://spotidoc.com/doc/1188035/mv-life-worth-living-essay-yale-center-for-faith-and-cu.

Chapter 12: Uncomfortable Unity

1. Wesley Hill, *Spiritual Friendship: Finding Love in the Church as a Celibate Gay Christian* (Grand Rapids, MI: Brazos Press, 2015), 36.

2. This is what Alan Kreider says in *The Patient Ferment of the Early Church: The Improbable Rise of Christianity in the Roman Empire* (Grand Rapids, MI: Baker Academic, 2016), 188, of these early Christian banquet meals: "All participants have to learn the habitus of the Christian banquet. The poor, who have never been at a banquet, need to learn the politesse and discipline of a meal. The richer members, who may have frequented an association's banquets, need to learn the values

of a community that does not seat people by rank but values the poor as equals. And all—poorer and richer—need to learn to share life and worship with people different from themselves."

3. Joseph A. Hellerman, *When the Church Was a Family* (Nashville: B&H Academic, 2009), 83, 87.

4. C. S. Lewis, *Mere Christianity* (San Francisco: HarperSanFrancisco, 2001), xv–xvi.

5. Ross Douthat, *Bad Religion: How We Became a Nation of Heretics* (New York: Free Press, 2012), 287.

6. John Piper, "Does 'Mere Christianity' Mean Eliminate Denominations?" Desiring God, October 1, 2013, http://www.desiringgod.org/articles/does -mere-christianity-mean-eliminate-denominations.

7. Douthat, *Bad Religion*, 153.

8. Cyprian of Carthage, "Letter 63," in *The Eucharist: Message of the Fathers of the Church*, ed. Daniel Sheerin (Wilmington, DE: Michael Glazier, 1986), 264.

Chapter 13: Uncomfortable Commitment

1. C. S. Lewis, *Mere Christianity* (San Francisco: HarperSanFrancisco, 2001), xv–xvi.

2. Wendy Wang and Kim Parker, "Record Share of Americans Have Never Married," Pew Research Center, September 24, 2014, http://www.pew socialtrends.org/2014/09/24/record-share-of-americans-have-never -married/.

3. Christena Cleveland, *Disunity in Christ: Uncovering the Hidden Forces That Keep Us Apart* (Downers Grove, IL: InterVarsity Press, 2013), 95.

4. Sam Allberry, *Why Bother with Church? And Other Questions about Why You Need It and Why It Needs You* (Epsom, UK: The Good Book Company, 2016), 23.

5. Joshua Ryan Butler, *The Pursuing God: A Reckless, Irrational, Obsessed Love That's Dying to Bring Us Home* (Nashville: W Publishing Group, 2016), 37.

6. Donald Miller, "I Don't Worship God by Singing. I Connect with Him Elsewhere." *Storyline* (blog), February 3, 2014, http://storylineblog .com/2014/02/03/i-dont-worship-god-by-singing-i-connect-with-him -elsewhere/.

7. Sarah Pulliam Bailey, "Rob Bell, the Pastor Who Questioned Hell, Is Now Surfing, Working with Oprah and Loving Life in L.A.," *The Huffington Post*, December 2, 2014, http://www.huffingtonpost.com/2014/12/02/rob -bell-oprah_n_6256454.html.

8. R. C. Sproul, *The Soul's Quest for God: Satisfying the Hunger for Spiritual Communion with God* (Carol Stream, IL: Tyndale, 1992), 151.

9. C. H. Spurgeon, "The Head and the Body," No. 2653, delivered Aug. 6, 1882 at Metropolitan Tabernacle, http://www.spurgeongems.org/vols43 -45/chs2653.pdf.

10. Allberry, *Why Bother with Church?*, 31.
11. Ross Douthat, *Bad Religion: How We Became a Nation of Heretics* (New York: Free Press, 2012), 236.
12. Ibid., 241.
13. Pope Francis, "Amoris Laetitia," 29, https://www.documentcloud.org/documents/2793677-AL-INGLESE-TESTO.html.
14. Jeanne Meister, "Job Hopping Is the 'New Normal' for Millennials: Three Ways to Prevent a Human Resource Nightmare," *Forbes*, August 14, 2012, http://www.forbes.com/sites/jeannemeister/2012/08/14/job-hopping-is-the-new-normal-for-millennials-three-ways-to-prevent-a-human-resource-nightmare/#6e455d9a5508.
15. David Brooks, "The Cultural Value of Christian Higher Education," *CCCU Advance* 7, no. 1, http://advance.cccu.org/stories/the-cultural-value-of-christian-higher-education.

Chapter 14: Countercultural Comfort

1. Rod Dreher, *The Benedict Option: A Strategy for Christians in a Post-Christian Nation* (New York: Sentinel, 2017), 101–2.
2. Brett McCracken, "Can Hipster Christianity Save Churches from Decline?" *Washington Post*, July 27, 2015, https://www.washingtonpost.com/news/acts-of-faith/wp/2015/07/27/can-hipster-christianity-save-churches-from-decline/.
3. This list of Christ's "paradoxical" teachings is from R. Kent Hughes, *The Sermon on the Mount: The Message of the Kingdom*, Preaching the Word (Wheaton, IL: Crossway, 2001), 33.

General Index

Scripture Index